Richer Descriptions

Gary A. Burlingame

Richer Descriptions

Gary A. Burlingame

What Will You Learn?

The sense of smell is a powerful sense – closely linked to your emotions and memory. Thus, smells influence your mood as well as your mental awareness. You rely on your sense of smell more than you think – you are constantly sniffing and sending messages to your brain whether you are aware of them or not.

Did you ever notice the aroma of a man's cologne or a woman's perfume as they passed you by on the street? How long did the fragrance persist? What did you smell as they moved past? Did the aroma change with distance? Was the aroma over-powering or was it a tease to your sense of smell?

God Himself speaks (2 Kings 18:12) and hears (2 Kings 19:16). God's voice thunders, breaks cedar trees, and is powerful (Ps. 29:3-5). The idols of wood and stone that people made could not speak, see, hear, smell, feel or touch (Ps. 115:4-7). But our God has always watched and listened to His people, smelling their sweet sacrifices and walking among them. Worship is a time of hearing. We hear the voices of God's people singing praises, shouting for joy and even weeping. We hear the Word preached and the declarations of faith from those who are saved.

You can hear the sound that rubber soles make on wood flooring, pressed down by over-weight or slender bodies. Listen as leather soled shoes pass by. Do they slap the wood or shuffle or slide? Do they sound different on marble than on tile flooring? Listen as the librarian opens a metal drawer, glides across the floor on the rollers of an old wooden office chair to speak in a low voice over the telephone.

The skin is the body's largest sensory organ – it has receptors for touch, pressure, pain, and temperature. Sensory information is provided by nerve endings in the skin's surface and deeper tissue, hair follicles, sweat glands, and blood vessels. The greatest number of receptors belongs to the nerves which give you the sense of pain.

The face is critical for communication and the development of relationships. Facial expressions affect your social comfort as well as your security and success. Thus, facial muscles have been mapped to help us better understand expression.

As you age, the cells that produce pigment die off and your hair loses its color. As a result, gray hair grows in, and can give way to white hair. The timing is largely a genetic factor. Some people gray early in life. Hair color changes after a person dies. In fact, brown and black pigments degrade faster such that a deceased person's hair will become redder in color.

For Deborah –
my loving wife and sensory companion

Richer Descriptions

Copyright © 2011, 2013 by Gary A. Burlingame

Published by:
Healthy Life Press, LLC; 2603 Drake Drive; Orlando, FL 32810
www.healthylifepress.com

Illustrations Copyright © 2011
by Marsha McCanney

Printed in the United States of America

No part of this publication may be reproduced, stored in a retrieval system, or transmitted in any form or by any means – for example, electronic, photocopy, recording – without the prior written permission of the author, except for brief quotations in printed reviews.

Library of Congress Cataloging-in-Publication Data
Burlingame, Gary A.
Richer Descriptions

ISBN 978-1-939267-32-0

1. Reference; 2. Writing Skills; 3. Speaking Skills

Most Healthy Life Press resources are available in printed or electronic forms worldwide through bookstores and online outlets, depending on their format. This book also exists in a downloadable and printable eBook PDF format from www.healthylifepress.com. Distribution of printed or eBook formatted copies, regardless of their source, without written authorization violates international copyright law, and is strictly forbidden.

Undesignated Scripture references are taken from the Holy Bible, New International Version®. Copyright © 1973, 1978, 1984 by the International Bible Society. Used by permission. All rights reserved. Scriptures marked KJV are from the King James Version of the Bible. Scriptures marked NASB are from the New American Standard Bible. Copyright © 1960, 1962, 1963, 1968, 1971, 1972, 1973, 1975, 1977 by the Lockman Foundation. Used by permission. All rights reserved.

CONTENTS

Preface   11

1
Created for a Sensory Experience   15
Just Imagine   17
More Than Five Senses   21
Help for Writers and Speakers   25

2
Understanding Flavor   35
Taste, Flavor and Aroma   39
The Nose and Tongue   45
Sweet, Salty, Sour and Bitter   49
Taste and Discernment   57
A Pleasing Aroma   59

3
How Smell Affects Our Lives   63
Perfume   67
Emotion-evoking Aromas   73
The Smell of Death, Disease, and Sin   77
The Anointed One   83
Environmental Fragrancing   87
Incense is Something Burned   91
Clothing and Building Materials   95

4
Describing Beverages, Spices and Fish 99
A Sip of Water 103
Coffee's Aroma 107
The Lure of Spices 111
Time for Tea 115
The Bouquet of Wine 119
The Body of a Good Beer 123
Off Flavors in Fish 127
There will be a Feast 131

5
Sound and Body Balance 135
Understanding Audition 139
Faith Comes by Hearing 143
The Ear and Body Balance 145
Where to Find Sounds of Life 149
Help in Describing Sounds 153

6
Touch, Pain, and Expressions 161
Touch is Very Important 165
Pain is Quite Complex 169
Healing Powers 175
Body Tremors 177
Facial Expressions 181
Daily Rhythms of the Body 185

7
Vision and Appearance 191
Understanding Vision   195
Light of the World   199
Describing Eyes and Hair   201
Skin Color   205
Where to Watch People   209

~

Chapter Notes   215

Index   223

Healthy Life Press Resources   230

PREFACE

At a fiction writers' luncheon I gave an overview of the human senses of taste and smell based on my more than twenty years of scientific experience. My fellow writers enjoyed the topic so much they encouraged me to put it in writing. With this encouragement I started to write about all nine human senses. After two years I had enough material for a book. Then my editor and publisher encouraged me to weave into the book my many notes on Bible references to the human senses. This made my book complete, and gave it the purpose for which I was searching.

Scientists continue to study and explore the human senses, to unlock its mysteries because they know how dependent we are, consciously and subconsciously, on our sensory systems for life's pleasures as well as for warnings of danger. Thus, it should be of no surprise that sensory imagery helps to bring alive the characters and scenes of your stories, or to awaken your audience when you are speaking. Whether for writing fiction, nonfiction or fantasy, the same holds true. Thus, this book's purpose is to better equip you with an understanding of the human senses and how they can be used to engage your audiences in a deeper and richer experience.

Richer Descriptions

A Guide to the Human Senses for Christian Speakers and Writers

Created For A Sensory Experience 1

MORE THAN 5 SENSES?

Just Imagine

Imagine going to church on a Saturday or Sunday morning. You park your car beneath a willow's shade and walk toward a stone church that proclaims that God is the rock of your life. In front, evergreen trees of various sizes and textures proclaim that Jesus is the way to eternal life. Down a path of lilies of all kinds and colors, you are reminded that your Lord cares for you more than the lilies of the field. An open door welcomes you inside where a deacon anoints your feet with spikenard, an anointing oil, because Jesus became a servant for you. Deeper inside, beneath a stone arch, another deacon sprays your outer garments with a mist of myrrh, aloes and cassia: the scent of the prophets and the priests, of which Christ is chief among them. Fragrant sandalwood, cedar, and acacia crafted pews, flooring, and altar catch the light of the morning sun streaming through an ornate stained glass window. The choir, accompanied by flute and harp, fill the sanctuary with David's Psalms, which touch on every emotion known to mankind. Out the north side windows you see a grove of apple trees and recall that you are among the people of God, the bride of Christ. Out the south-side windows you see a grove of fig trees and recall the beauty of creation, and yet Jesus died on a tree to redeem His creation. The offering plate, its cedar bottom scented with aloes, passes through your hands as you return your tithe with gladness of heart.

The sick move forward to receive healing balm amid prayers from the elders. Others are anointed with olive oil before they kneel at the prayer altar where perfumed incense (frankincense and galbanum) fills the air, rising with their prayers toward heaven where Jesus now sits at the right hand of His Father.

The ceiling is painted with birds and clouds, and toward the back with stars, for God made the earth in six days and on the seventh day He rested.

You receive a cup of the most wonderfully balanced and aged red wine – children receive clusters of sweet red grapes. Everyone receives bread dipped in honey, for His Word is sweeter than honey. The priest recites the Word of God from both Old and New Testaments, and expounds while you meditate. A crescendo of worship rises as everyone joins in unison, singing hymns.

On the way out of the sanctuary, a deacon hands you a bag of salt to encourage you to persevere through the week and to be salt for the world, for the glory of God. Outside you stand in the warm sun and greet others with the touch of kindness, celebrating God's blessings through the fellowship of believers. Back at home, at the end of the day, you join with your spouse in prayer, reading together from the Song of Solomon. Can you imagine what that would be like?

Write an Outline to Practice Speaking on *Making Sense of the Bible* using the following Bible verses:

- Genesis 6:11
- Genesis 3:9
- Psalm 34:8
- Isaiah 6:8-10
- Amos 8:11-12
- Matthew 5:14
- Matthew 14:35-36
- Mark 8:22-25
- Luke 14:12-24
- Romans 10:17
- 1 Corinthians 12:14-26
- James 1:22-25
- 1 John 1:5-7
- Revelation 3:15-16

The Lord's Supper, or communion sacrament, that is a memorial to the birth, life, death, and resurrection of our Lord Jesus Christ is itself a sensory experience. Communion is centered on the breaking of bread and the drinking of wine. The bread symbolizes His body or flesh (we share in His temptations, suffering, punishment, condemnation). The wine symbolizes His blood (we share in His judgment, atonement, and death). We must consume and taste of His suffering and humanity to truly accept His grace and be filled with the joy that goes beyond suffering.

Consider how Christ used wine to symbolize His blood sacrifice (Mark 14: 22-25). Jesus turned the water into wine at the wedding feast of Cana. Wine is sweet and drinking it makes the heart glad. To make wine you must pluck the fruit from the vine and crush it to release its juice (the blood of the grape as in Gen. 49:11). Then it is fermented and aged to maturity. Wine is the fruit of the vine. Jesus has been described as the vine, and we as the branches who produce the fruit that bear the fragrance of Christ.

In John 6 we read that Jesus is the bread of life. The Passover Feast is rich in symbolism as it commemorates God's delivery of Israel from slavery. Passover reminds us that the blood of the lamb protected the Jews from God's wrath. Passover makes symbolic use of bread. Leaven is a symbol for sin in both the Old and New Testaments. There was no leaven used in sacrificial offerings as Christ (the Lamb of God) had no sin. Since bread is made by crushing kernels of grain to make flour, so our hard outer shells must be broken and removed to make us fit for daily service.

The communion table is a feast – a delight to the senses . . . not just a physical tease of the senses but a spiritual wonder. We will not taste death (Matt. 16:28; Heb. 2:9) since death has lost its sting for those in Christ. As we taste the bread and the wine, we taste the victory of Christ over sin and death.

As the Bible calls us to remembrance, so it also calls us to look forward to when Christ comes again. Though we cannot go back in time, we can look forward with eagerness to the new heaven and new earth. The Garden of Eden must have been a truly wonderful place. Nothing was harmful. Nothing was bitter or sour to repel the taste. Nothing in the Garden was foul smelling; no odor of decay. Fragrant aromas filled the moist atmosphere. Fruits of various trees provided a gourmet's delight of flavors. The visual beauty was inspiring. The sound of the birds in every tree provided a continuous choir. The textures were stimulating, as everything was safe to touch and explore. Let us, therefore, enjoy our senses until that time comes when we enter into the presence of Christ and worship Him with all our capacity – until we return to the sensory paradise of His most excellent creation.

More than Five Senses

There are five well-recognized senses: taste, smell, vision, hearing, and touch. But sensory perception involves more than just the eyes, ears, nose, mouth, and fingers. **Scientists and medical experts today define nine senses**, not just five. These include the senses of pain, temperature, joint position, muscle position, movement, vibrations, and gravity. In general, **exteroception** senses (such as sight and hearing) keep us in touch with our environment, whereas **interoception** senses (cutaneous, kinesthetic, vestibular) keep us in touch with our bodies. The somatosensory system (soma means body) includes the cutaneous sense (body temperature, pain, visceral sensations, inflammation, itching) which uses receptors in the skin and gives us the sense of touch and pain.

The kinesthetic sense uses sensory receptors and neurons in muscles and mobile joints such as the knees, elbows, and shoulders. These receptors detect the body's position and movement, as in the positioning of your arms and legs. This helps you judge weight because it takes body position and muscles to hold something up against gravity. The kinesthetic sense is highly trained by gymnasts, skaters, ballet dancers, and weight lifters.

EXAMPLE

He had an uncanny way of moving about the house. He sensed the squeaky floor boards with the soles of his feet. He climbed the stairs, with his toes clinging to the edge where the stairs were solid – all this in the darkness. The settling of the house in the cooling of the night made more sound than his movement about the house – and this unnerved me.

Did you ever wonder how a baseball player can throw a pitch to a batter or run deep into left field to catch a fly ball? The vestibular sense keeps him in balance, and helps him to sense direction of movement and speed. The integration of the kinesthetic sense (of body movement) with equilibrioception (the vestibular sense) creates a sense called **proprioception**. This is the sense of body awareness. This integrated sense allows you to accomplish complicated tasks such as walking with your eyes closed while reaching for a doorknob. A dysfunction of the proprioception sense, or the processing of sensory information, would cause you to be clumsy, uncoordinated, and accident-prone.

We all learn by using our senses, but how you use your senses to learn might be different than how your brother, sister, spouse, or friend uses senses to learn. Some of us learn by listening (auditory learners) or seeing (visual learners). Some need to touch (tactile) or do something (kinesthetic) to make the experience take root. Many of us use a variety of these means of learning rather than just relying on any one sense.

Sensory adaptation occurs when continuous stimulation results in a loss of awareness or loss in the detection of changes that stimulate our sensory receptors. Have you ever worn a hat for a long time, and after a while you forgot you were still wearing it? Your senses adapted to the feeling of the hat.

EXAMPLE

The cycling hum-rum-hum-rum-hum of the generator stopped. It was two in the morning. The aging foreman didn't seem to notice. I peeked into his ear to see if he was wearing ear plugs. Maybe he didn't care anymore? Or maybe he was testing me! An hour later I asked if the generator was supposed to go silent. "What?" he screamed at me. "Why didn't you tell me! You idiot! I've been down here so many years I can't hear it anymore, and I don't notice when it shuts down."

Synesthesia is where one of the senses stimulates another sense. Though all your senses are interlinked in amazing ways, synesthesia is a condition where senses overlap – for example, you hear sound but envision a color or shape or pattern. Colored hearing is the most common form of this disorder.

Your senses will weaken with age – hearing and vision tend to decrease with age more quickly than the sense of smell. Senses are also affected by diseases, medicine, and injuries. A loss in sensory ability may predict the onset of a disease. For example, the loss of smell is one predictor of Alzheimer's Disease. A loss of sensory ability could also be followed by other problems. For example, a loss of smell could result in poor eating habits, weight loss, and poor nutrition which in turn could lead to depression.

The following chapters describe the human senses and their use in greater detail. As a writer or speaker, I hope you'll develop a better understanding of the human senses and how they can be used to enrich your audience's experience. Diane Ackerman wrote, "One of the real tests of writers, especially poets, is how well they write about smell." Most importantly, God desires for us to experience Him with our senses. It was God who gave us our senses (Ex. 4:11). The idols of wood and stone that people made could not speak, see, hear, smell, feel, or touch (Ps. 115:4-7). But the God that we know has always watched and listened to His people, smelling their sweet sacrifices and walking among them. When Jesus appeared to His disciples after rising from the dead, they thought He was a ghost, but He told them to touch Him, see Him, hear Him and behold His appearance (Luke 24:37-40).

Help for Writers and Speakers

The Summary of Our Sensory Systems is a quick reference table. It is not set up to be a working guide for writing or speaking. This is the purpose of the **Speakers' Checklist** and the **Guide to Use of Sensory Descriptions in a Scene**.

The **Summary of Our Sensory Systems** brings together the nine senses. These nine senses provide sensory experiences, such as flavor when consuming beverages by mouth. Flavor is an integration of several sensory systems including taste, smell, and touch.

Not shown in the table is the integrated sense of proprioception, which provides your awareness of your body in the space around it. This sense can be highly trained, as with a gymnast or a golfer, allowing them to make and plan complex movements. This summary table places all nine senses in context.

The **Guide to Use of Sensory Descriptions in a Scene** is a guide for writers. **The Speakers' Checklist** is a guide for speakers. Both include helpful hints in a worksheet format.

A blank checklist and guide are included, and can be copied for use by you over and over again as you work through your scenes and prepare your talks. You might use them to help set up an outline or a scene before writing it. You might use the Writer's Guide after you have a first or second draft complete, as a check to make sure that the sensory imagery you wanted to use was incorporated.

Summary of Our Sensory Systems

Sensory System	Common Name	Sensory Receptor
Olfaction	Smell	Smell is detected by the olfactory bulb in the nose. Orthonasal smell occurs when air directly enters the nose. Retronasal smell occurs when air rises from the mouth and throat up the back passageway to the nose.
Gustation	Taste	Taste buds on the tongue, as well as throughout the mouth and throat, detect the basic tastes sweet, salty, sour, bitter, and umami (Japanese for "meaty".)
Tactile Sense	Touch	Skin has nerves and hairs that detect pressure, vibration, and the stretching of skin. There are receptors on the outer skin as well as inside the body.
Thermoception	Hot & Cold	Hot and cold are detected by separate receptors in the skin.
Nociception	Pain	Receptors in the skin differentiate between acute, sharp pain, and lasting, dull pain, as well as chronic pain by way of the brain's memory.
Audition	Hearing	Ears differentiate and recognize sound and its direction.
Vision	Sight	Eyes differentiate color, light, patterns, and dimension.
Equilibrioception	Balance	The inner ear's vestibular system keeps the body in balance.
Kinesthetic Sense	Position and Movement	Muscles, tendons, ligaments, and joints have receptors to support body movement and the position of arms and legs.

Speakers' Checklist for Engaging an Audience through Sensory Experiences

Topic: _____

Sensory Aspects to Consider
(circle the ones of interest):

Smell	Touch	Taste
Hot/Cold	Pain	Hearing
Sight	Balance	Position/Movement

Questions to Ask Yourself

- How might these senses relate in general to the topic of my talk?

- How might my personal experiences through my senses relate to my topic?

- What does the Bible say about these senses, and how does God use them to share spiritual truth?

- What are some ways in which I can draw on my audience's personal experience using these senses, to engage them deeper in my message or story?

The **Speakers' Checklist** is quite simple. When preparing your outline for a speaking engagement, and when rehearsing your talk, you can check off which senses you might consider elaborating on. You can run through the checklist to help decide how the human senses, or how descriptions of sensory experiences, might engage your audience at a deeper level. You might even use the checklist to consider what visuals to use, how the room should be arranged, whether to play background music, and how to dress. If you can incorporate one or more sensory experiences into your talk, your audience will be drawn into your story or your subject matter more intimately. Don't underestimate the power of the human senses on both personal and group experiences. Use sensory clues and descriptions, appropriately, to enhance your message and your story.

Here is an example of the use of the **Guide to Use of Sensory Descriptions in a Scene** for a scene where an elderly man befriends a stray dog. The man is aged, and therefore has diminished sensory abilities such as smell, balance, sight, and hearing. These diminished senses affect his sensory experience with the stray dog. The initial draft of this scene might read like this:

EXAMPLE

Tom sat on the wooden crate, a cup of iced tea in his hand, his eyes drooping from the heat of the afternoon. A stray dog had been watching him for some time, like trying to place an old friend. Tom finished the tea and placed the cup on the ground, motioning to the dog. The stray approached Tom slowly. The stray sniffed at the cup and began licking the ice cubes. Tom tried to pet the stray, but the dog jumped backward and Tom stood. The two stared each other out, waiting for the next move.

The second draft might read like this, after using the Guide to add more sensory imagery:

> **EXAMPLE (rewritten)**
>
> *Old Tom sat on the wooden crate, his knees throbbing, a cup of iced tea in his arthritic left hand, his back bowed against the brick wall and his eyes drooping from the heat of the afternoon. A stray dog in desperate need of a bath was watching him for some time, like trying to place an old friend. The dog was upwind and could not smell Tom, who finished the tasteless tea and placed the cup on the ground, motioning to the dog. The stray approached Tom slowly. Tom closed his eyes. He could not smell the stray, but he could hear the dog's panting coming closer. The stray sniffed at the cup and began licking the ice cubes. Tom pealed his eyelids open to a slit as his shaky hand slipped off his lap. There was a collar around the dog's neck, but Tom could not make out any imprints on it. As he tried to pet the stray, he brushed its cold wet nose. The stray jumped backward and Tom stood up, teetering. They stared at each other, waiting for the next move.*

Together with the summary table and guides, this book explains in greater detail the human senses with examples of sensory imagery.

Guide to Use of Sensory Descriptions in a Scene

Character's Attributes Age: _____ Gender: _____ Health Status: _____

Sensory System	Character's Health Status			Sensory Descriptions used in this scene will describe:			
	Healthy	Not Normal	Injured, Diseased	Environmental or Living Thing	Food, Drink, or Air	Another Person	Oneself
Smell							
Taste							
Touch							
Hot/Cold							
Pain							
Hearing							
Sight							
Balance							
Body Awareness							

Guide to Use of Sensory Descriptions in a Scene: Elderly man befriends a stray dog

Character's Attributes Age: 75   Gender: M   Health Status: Normal for his age

Sensory System	Character's Health Status			Sensory Descriptions used in this scene will describe:			
	Healthy	Not Normal	Injured Diseased	Environmental or Living Thing	Food, Drink, or Air	Another Person	Oneself
Smell			Aging	Can't smell the dog			Wonders if the dog smells him
Taste					Sips iced tea		
Touch				Pets the dog			
Hot/Cold			Aging				Eyelids close and open
Pain				Dog's nose is cold			Arthritis in hands, knees
Hearing			Aging	Dog pants			
Sight			Aging	Dog looks like it needs a bath			Watches hands pet the dog
Balance			Aging	Plays with dog			Stands and sits
Body Awareness			Aging				Dog might jump up on him

2
Understanding Flavor

Charles Dickens – *A Christmas Carol*

They left the high road, by a well-remembered lane, and soon approached a mansion of dull red brick, with a little weather cock-surmounted cupola, on the roof, and a bell hanging in it. It was a large house, but one of broken fortunes; for the spacious offices were little used, their walls were damp and mossy, their windows broken, and their gates decayed. Fowls clucked and strutted in the stables, and the coach-houses and sheds were overrun with grass. Nor was it more retentive of its ancient state, within; for entering the dreary hall, and glancing through the open doors of many rooms, they found them poorly furnished, cold, and vast. There was an earthy savor in the air, a chilly bareness in the place, which associated itself somehow with too much getting up by candle-light, and not too much to eat.

(Mahweh, NJ: Watermill Press, 1980), 37-38.

Taste, Flavor, and Aroma

> **EXAMPLE**
>
> She tasted the melted milk chocolate. Its sweetness reminded her of a lost love, of love lost.

Flavor involves multiple senses: olfactory (smell); gustatory (taste); thermal (hot, cold); pain; and texture (feeling). These senses are very important to the enjoyment of everyday life such that a loss of smell can bring about depression or poor nutrition.

> **EXAMPLE**
>
> She passed him on the street. Her perfume trailed behind, fading from a strong floral scent to a mysterious muskiness. He turned to watch her slip away into the crowd.

"**Taste**" is a very general term as it is often used. Scientifically, however, taste refers to sweet, salty, sour, and bitter sensations from the taste buds in the mouth, most of which are found on the tongue. Some people are "super-tasters" – they have a higher density of taste buds on their tongue, which gives them a heightened sensitivity to the taste of bitter. An example of a **sweet** taste comes from sucrose or sugar. An example of a **salty** taste comes from table salt or sodium chloride. An example of a **sour** taste comes from citric acid, as found in lemon juice. An example of **bitter** comes from caffeine. There is a fifth taste, known as "umami" (or **savory**). It is a Japanese term and comes from the meaty, protein-like sensation enhanced by the use of monosodium glutamate (MSG), which can be readily noticed in fish sauces, mushrooms, some cheeses, soy sauce, cured meats, and broths.

EXAMPLE

Beer was, like life itself, something that he could never enjoy – his hypersensitivity to things bitter enhanced his negative outlook on his friends, work, church, getting older, and love itself.

"**Flavor**" is a broad term that encompasses taste, odor, and feelings as sensed when consuming a food or beverage by mouth. **Feelings** (such as mouth feel and nose feel) are triggered by the trigeminal nerve. Your nose, mouth, and associated passageways are lined with nerve endings that provide feeling sensations such as spicy hot, slick, drying, astringent, and crispy.

EXAMPLE

She watched him sip the glass of Shiraz. Would its flavor fill his senses with its refined balance of wonderfully aged aroma? Could he savor her love as well?

Aroma or odor, the smell of something, occurs in two ways. First, when you inhale or sniff through your nose you pull in odorous air that ascends up to your olfactory bulb. **Retronasal** sensations of odor occur when you chew, sip, slurp, and swallow and the released odors rise up through the back passageway from your throat to your nose, allowing you to smell what you swallowed. You enjoy most foods by smelling retronasally and not by sniffing them with your nose as a dog might do.

> **EXAMPLE**
>
> *The boxer chewed his dinner with little enthusiasm. His broken, swollen nose forced him to breathe through his mouth as he ate. Tony's special, garlic chicken with cheesy pasta, tasted like wet paper.*

If you want to experience **retronasal smell**, try tasting or drinking a flavorful beverage with your nose pinched. The elimination of nasal airflow prevents your olfactory bulb from sensing any odors. Then release your nose while closing your mouth and breathing through your nose. This brings air flow up from your mouth and into your nose. You will experience a burst of smell as the odors from your mouth flow up to the olfactory center in your nose.

> **EXAMPLE**
>
> *Her mother stared at the meatloaf on her plate for several minutes. Then with anger she shook the salt at the meal as if a loss of smell was the reason she was in the nursing home.*

Some people can be "blind" to the smell of certain chemicals or odors (they just can't smell), or they might have a weakened sensitivity to certain odors (they can smell odors but only at high concentrations). A loss of smell can happen from brain damage or from a virus that has infected the olfactory system. However, everyone experiences a diminished sense of smell ability with age. Women who are pregnant tend to be hyperosmotic or hypersensitive to smell. "Anosmia" is where a person cannot smell odors. "Parosmia" is where the sense of smell is distorted as when a good odor is perceived to be sickening. "Phantosmia" is where the brain signals an odor that is not really there. People who lose their sense of smell, however, may still sense chemicals that give rise to odors because there are chemicals (such as ammonia and vinegar) that elicit feeling sensations or nose feel (burning, drying, stinging) that can be detected even when the odor cannot be smelled.

The sense of smell is a powerful sense – closely linked to your emotions and memory. Thus, smells influence your mood and emotional state, as well as your mental awareness. You rely on your sense of smell more than you think – you are constantly sniffing and sending messages to your brain whether you are aware of it or not.

> **EXAMPLE**
>
> *Opening the door to his apartment, he stood motionless for some time, searching the living room to see if any object was out of place, listening for any unusual sound, and smelling for any out-of-place scent. He turned his head to the left and sniffed, then to the right and sniffed. What was that smell? Aha! He remembered. He had smelled that same odor in the court room, when the defense attorney had approached the stand, shaking his stubby finger at him and claiming that he could not have witnessed the murder on that rainy Tuesday night.*

Did you ever stop to think about how you use your sense of smell in everyday life? It happens without thinking until something triggers "danger" or a memory. When you enter a room you employ your sense of smell without thinking about it (unless it's a coffee shop or a bakery). You smell to compare what you experience to what you expected to experience (when you enter a bakery you expect to smell baked goods) or a past experience (when you come home from work, you expect your home to smell the same way as when you left it.) If it meets your expectations, you continue without thinking. If you detect a difference, you try to identify the difference (such as by naming the odor or associating the smell with something you know) in order to make a decision such as should you continue, or is there danger?

EXERCISE

The characters in your stories see, touch, and hear – they also taste and smell. One way to help you enhance this imagery is to keep a notebook of taste, smell, and flavor experiences. On each page of your notebook write: item, taste, mouthfeel, and smell. Start with hot soups, which have salty and sweet tastes and an aroma volatilized by the heat. For taste, pinch off your nose and sip. This will help minimize the aroma. Notice the tastes. Notice also feelings such as spicy, drying and hot. Then take a mouthful, and breathe through your nose and close your mouth. Notice the burst of aroma that ascends up to your olfactory bulb. Record your sensations and try another food or beverage. Chew on dry crackers and sip plain water to cleanse your palate between tasting.

The Nose and Tongue

In the Bible, the nose can be a feature of beauty, a source of life, or an instrument of judgment. In Genesis 24:47 and Ezekiel 16:12 we find that the bride's nose draws much attention. In 2 Kings 19:28 we read that the nose is defiled when a ring is put through it and man is made a slave.

> Write an Outline to Practice Speaking on *The Breath of God* using the following Bible verses:
>
> - Genesis 2:7
> - Genesis 7:22
> - Job 12:10
> - Job 27:3
> - Job 34:4
> - Psalm 146:4
> - Isaiah 2:22
> - Ezekiel 37:1-14
> - Lamentations 4:20

The nose is mentioned in Genesis 2:7 where God gave the breath of life through man's nose. To breathe life into man through his nose brought attention to the fact that life is derived from God and God is central to it (Job 12:10). And in turn, to please God we must become a sweet smell to His nostrils or the center of His being. The Bible restates the nose's significance in Song of Solomon 7:4.

> Write an Outline to Practice Speaking on *Being a Nosey Christian* using the following Bible verses:
>
> - Exodus 15:8
> - Numbers 11:18-20
> - 2 Samuel 22:9
> - 2 Samuel 22:16
> - Job 27:3
> - Job 41:20
> - Psalm 18:8
> - Psalm 18:15
> - Psalm 115:4-6
> - Proverbs 30:33
> - Isaiah 65:5
> - Ezekiel 8:17
> - Amos 4:10

The Lord God made man from the earth and breathed the breath of life through his nose. The Spirit is the breath of God, like a mighty wind. God's grace swirled and flowed through Adam's nasal passages. Was Adam imprinted with the scent of God? Do we have the inherent capability to discern the things that smell like God versus the things that smell of death? There can be no doubt that, in the Bible, significance has been given to this sensory organ that is used for smelling.

The nose is used numerous times in the Bible to describe God's anger (2 Sam. 22:16; Job 4:9; Isa. 65:5). Exodus 15:8 is an example: God gave five blasts out of His nose. In Nehemiah 9:17 and Psalm 103:8, we find God as slow to anger or "long-nosed." In Proverbs it is said that if you strike a man on his nose, he will bleed (Prov. 30:33).

The tongue can drip with honey, stick to one's mouth, burn in agony, or praise the Lord. The tongue (which is important for tasting foods as well as for speech) is the author of many sins and is sharp like a serpent. The Bible points out that the tongue can be a blessing or a curse (James 3:1-12).

Write an Outline to Practice Speaking on *Speaking of Tongues* using the following Bible verses:

- Judges 7:5
- Job 6:30
- Job 29:10
- Psalm 10:7
- Psalm 34:13
- Psalm 39:1
- Psalm 137:6
- Proverbs 6:16-17
- Proverbs 12:18
- Proverbs 15:2,4
- Song of Solomon 4:11
- Ezekiel 3:26
- Ezekiel 5:24
- Lamentations 4:4
- Mark 7:33-35
- Luke 16:24
- Romans 14:11
- Philippians 2:11
- Revelation 16:10

Sweet, Salty, Sour, and Bitter

Taste is the sense whereby you detect salty, sour, sweet and bitter, using taste buds scattered throughout your mouth but mainly on your tongue. While sweet tastes are often related to good things, such as milk and candy, bitter is associated with bad things, such as poison. Yet bitter tastes are important to the flavor of many of your favorite foods (such as chocolate) and beverages (such as coffee and beer). Caffeine's lingering bitter taste provides added benefits by helping to balance the overall flavor of beverages.

EXAMPLE

The inspector confirmed her story – the coffee was unusually strong in its bitter taste because it was laced with high levels of caffeine. This stimulant had caused her father's heart to speed up, become erratic, and eventually to fail altogether.

The Bible addresses four taste sensations: sweet, salty, sour, and bitter (or sweetness, sourness, saltiness, and bitterness). A sweet incense is a fragrant incense in the Bible. A sweet savor is also a soothing aroma. Different Bible versions use different wording. **The Word of God and wise loving counsel are sweet like honey** (Ps. 119:103; Prov. 16:24 and 24:13). As a child is trained to eat honey for his health, so we should train our children to enjoy the Word of God.

Sweet, on the other hand, causes a desire for more, and chocolate plays on this desire. You might have a "sweet tooth" for candy. Sweet tastes encourage you to feed on energy-rich carbohydrates, which in turn induce your body's release of chemicals that produce a feeling of calmness.

> Write an Outline to Practice Speaking on *Sweet Treats from the Bible* using the following Bible verses:
>
> - Exodus 15:25
> - Nehemiah 8:10
> - Psalm 19:10
> - Psalm 119:103
> - Proverbs 9:17
> - Proverbs 16:24
> - Proverbs 24:13
> - Song of Solomon 5:13
> - Song of Solomon 5:16
> - Isaiah 43:24
> - Amos 9:13
> - Revelation 10:9-10

Babies have sweet taste buds all over their mouths, giving them an intense desire for their mothers' milk (full of fat and sugar), providing nutrients for development and calories for growth, while reducing stress, crying, and metabolic rate to allow the calories to support rapid growth and development.

> ### EXAMPLE
>
> *Her innocent smile and sparkling eyes left me with a sweet aftertaste – a desire for more. It was candy to my soul.*

Genesis 27:34 lays a foundation for the Bible's reference to the bitter sensation. When Esau was spoken to by his father, he cried out with a bitter cry. Bitter relates to sorrow and judgment, and even to death (Deut. 32:32-33).

Bitter is part of the symbolism of Passover, the Jewish tradition that commemorates their freedom from Egypt. The Seder is on the first day of Passover. The Seder plate includes ground bitter herbs (such as horseradish) to represent the bitterness of slavery and to draw tears to the eyes when eaten. The historical context of Passover is the redemption of God's chosen people from their bitter bondage in Egypt, thus the eating of bitter herbs. Grief, pain, and sorrow are often said, poetically, to leave a bitter taste.

Write an Outline to Practice Speaking on *The Bitter Passages of the Bible* using the following Bible verses:

- Exodus 12:8
- Exodus 15:23
- Numbers 5:18
- Numbers 5:23-24
- Deuteronomy 32:32
- Job 3:20
- Proverbs 5:3-4
- Proverbs 27:7
- Ecclesiastes 7:26
- Isaiah 5:20
- Isaiah 24:9
- Jeremiah 2:19
- Acts 8:22-23
- Hebrews 12:15
- Revelation 8:11
- Revelation 10:9

Poisoned water is called water of gall as in Jeremiah 8:14, 9:15 and 23:15. Gall or bitter drink is recorded in the Bible (Job 16:13; Matt. 27:34). The word gall is interchanged with the word bitterness (Job 17:13; Matt. 27:34; Acts 8:22-23). A bitter taste is associated with poison or bad things as with Moses and the Pharaoh; bitter waters were a curse from God. Roman soldiers offered Jesus a drink of wine vinegar. It might have contained gall or myrrh, making it bitter. It was offered on the stalk of the hyssop plant (Mark 15:23).

There are experiences in life that leave us with a bitter taste in our mouths. Naomi asked to be called Mara because of the bitterness of her life (Ruth 1:20). In Romans 8:18-23 we find examples of the bitter taste of sin:
- we have present sufferings
- creation is subjected to frustration
- sin's bondage leads to decay
- we feel the pains of child birth
- we groan inwardly.

EXAMPLE

The chocolate store below my apartment appealed to my varying moods – today I desired a bitter, dark almond morsel to support my anger at the consequences of the life I had fallen into. Maybe tomorrow I'll stop by and treat myself to milk chocolate-covered strawberries – that is, if everything goes as planned.

Chocolate, really good chocolate, has a very careful blend of bitter and sweet tastes (from the cocoa and sugar). It comes from large cocoa pods, split open for the waxy and bitter cocoa beans. The beans are fermented and roasted and husked. They are ground with sugar, vanilla, cocoa butter, and soy lecithin and beaten slowly for hours to make a smooth fine powder. Then they are tempered by raising and lowering the temperature, to get the cocoa butter to crystallize so as to make the chocolate firm, to be poured into molds. High quality chocolate uses high quality cocoa beans, dairy butter, and quality cream. Dark baking chocolate is quite bitter tasting. Think of Jesus and how bitter was His death. He wept blood and endured the cross. Yet how sweet was His victory. Such a perfect blend of bitter and sweet no earthly chocolate could ever produce!

The Bible makes little use of salt, yet what it does say about salt is very profound. Genesis 19:26 is perhaps the most famous reference to salt in the Old Testament where Lot's wife became a pillar of salt. Salt had a variety of uses. For example, salt was applied to the wounds of the body after it was whipped in order to stop its bleeding and halt infection, as well as to sting the person who had been whipped back to consciousness.

> Write an Outline to Practice Speaking on *Walk the Talk with Salt* using the following Bible verses:
>
> - Leviticus 2:13
> - Numbers 18:19
> - 2 Chronicles 13:5
> - Matthew 5:13
> - Mark 9:49-50
> - Luke 14:34-35
> - Colossians 4:6
> - James 3:11

God's Word is like salt – bringing flavor to our lives. Matthew 5:13-16 tells us to be the salt of the earth, but a salt that remains useful (Mark 9:50). When salt is pure, it is clear and of high quality for foods, and it is good to be consumed. This salt was valuable and was traded. Salt evaporated from the sea has a lot of impurities that diminish its use and value. A salt that had lost its purity was thrown away (Luke 34). We are called to redeem or transform the world; not to just prevent deterioration (as a salt preservative) but to bring out the flavor (transform the culture, glorify God).

The sensation of sour has very little use throughout the Bible. Nurtured grapes have a greater content of sugar and so they taste sweet. Wild grapes taste sour. The Promised Land had large, sweet grapes. The Bible often refers to eating sour grapes or to the complaining of the people of God (Jer. 31:29-30). Children who grew up during the years of captivity became angry because they had to live with the repercussions of their forefathers' sins – they had to eat sour grapes. But Jesus tasted sour wine on our behalf so that we might enjoy the finest of sweet wines, as presented to us through His atonement.

Write an Outline to Practice Speaking on *Has the Bible Gone Sour?* using the following Bible verses:

- Psalm 69:21
- Jeremiah 31:29-30
- Ezekiel 18:1-4
- Matthew 27:48

YOUR TURN

Finish the scene:

It's Valentine's Day! He won't embarrass me again in front of my co-workers. I'll make him a gift box that will . . .

Taste and Discernment

To taste can also mean to enjoy, eat, feel, or experience. In 1 Peter 2:2-3 we are to taste that the Lord is gracious and experience Him firsthand (Heb. 6:4-6). Revelation 3:16 is a warning to those who are "neither hot nor cold" (who are insipid or tasteless).

The use of the term "taste" can refer to "flavor" (the whole of the sensory experience when consuming a food or beverage). Wine is a good example of this: Wine can taste sweet, sour, or bitter but has a bouquet of many aromas. Wine has been used as a symbol of God's Spirit and grace to us (Hosea 14:7). Jesus' first public miracle turned water into wine. The Last Supper involved wine. When Jesus hung on the cross the Roman soldiers offered Him wine vinegar. Jesus said that He is the vine and we are the branches, and we are to produce good fruit. We are to enjoy God's blessings (Gen. 27:28; Deut. 7:13; Amos 9:13) and have our spirits lifted (Esther 1:10; Ps. 104:15; Eccl. 9:7) as we would experience by drinking good wine.

When we taste food to decide if we like it or not, we make a decision based on a reference. Nothing is neutral. Similarly, as God draws us to Himself we respond to His influence over other influences – over Satan, the world, and our flesh. The mention of fruit, nuts, and other foods in the Bible often has a deeper spiritual meaning. In Judges 9:7-15 we find references to a good king (a vine, olive, fig) and a bad king (a thorn bush). The good king gives up his life by being crushed (as grapes or olives give up their sweetness) or by being broken open (as with the fig). The bad king refuses to be broken.

We are called in Matthew 5:13 to be salt of the earth – salt that brings forth flavor, emphasizing both desirable and undesirable qualities. There is a fruit that is commonly known as "miracle fruit." It comes from a small tropical African tree. The fruit contains a glycoprotein that causes sour/bitter substances to taste sweet; it takes the unpalatable and makes it desirable.

We need to exercise our senses (Job 12:11) or we could become anosmic and undiscerning. As we grow in the Lord we are to train our tastes such as to recognize the bitter and the sweet. Satan's desire would be to confuse or deaden our discernment (Isa. 5:20).

Write an Outline to Practice Speaking on *The Bible's Guide to Taste Testing* using the following Bible verses:

- Exodus 16:31
- Numbers 11:4-9
- 1 Samuel 14:29
- 1 Samuel 14:43
- 2 Samuel 19:35
- Job 6:6
- Job 12:11
- Psalm 34:8
- Psalm 119:103
- Proverbs 24:13
- Song of Solomon 2:3
- Jeremiah 48:11
- Matthew 16:28
- Matthew 27:34
- Luke 14:24
- John 8:52
- Colossians 2:20-21
- Hebrews 6:4-6
- 1 Peter 2:2-3

A Pleasing Aroma

The sense of smell throughout the Old and New Testaments sometimes presents a pleasing aroma, as of life, and sometimes a foul odor, as of death. In 2 Corinthians 2:15-16, we read that when we accept Jesus Christ as our Savior we acquire the "sweet savor of Christ." On the other hand, sin is a vile odor and associated with odors of death and decay (Judges 3:22-25; Ex. 5:21 and 7:18).

In 2 Corinthians 2:14-17 there appear four aspects to aroma: (1) the knowledge of Him; (2) the aroma of Christ; (3) the smell of death; (4) the fragrance of life. We are to give off the knowledge of Christ like a sweet aroma, pure and undefiled. This passage represents our association with Christ in His triumph. He manifests through us the sweet aroma, which is the knowledge of Him. We give off the fragrance of Christ because we have been justified by Christ. Jesus Christ is to be the perfume that we pour upon our heads to fill our nostrils and to fragrance the air around us (Song of Solomon 1:2-4).

Christ became our sacrifice – a burnt offering on the altar, pleasing to God. As we give off the knowledge of Christ, it rises like a sweet aroma, pleasing to God. Sacrifices or offerings that are not pleasing to God have a displeasing smell (Eccl. 10:1; Joel 2:20). Pleasing sacrifices have a fragrant smell (Ex. 29:18; Lev. 1:9, 1:13, 1:17, 2:9, 3:5, 3:16 and 4:31). The bad smell of our sin drives God away, thus we need the sweet aroma of a sacrificial substitute to draw God back (Gen. 8:21).

It is known that our ability to smell decreases with age – this has been proven by scientific methods. The Bible described this in 2 Samuel 19:31-37 when eighty-year-old Barzillai the Gileadite came from Rogelim to cross the Jordan with the king. Barzillai lamented about his age to the king, emphasizing that he had few years of life left and his sense of taste (or smell) was gone, and his hearing faded. As we age and approach death, perhaps, our senses become weaker and we become less discerning and more accepting of things we should not allow in our lives.

The fragrance of Christ is life to some but death to others. Here, odor carries an association with life and death. The aroma of the knowledge of God can be a life-sustaining fragrance to those who accept Christ. But to those who do not, it is an aroma of death, for God uses the knowledge of Christ to convict.

Write an Outline to Practice Speaking on *The Sweet Aroma of Christ* using the following Bible verses:

- Genesis 27:26-27
- Leviticus 6:15
- Leviticus 8:21-29
- Leviticus 17:6
- Leviticus 26:31
- Numbers 18:17
- Psalm 45:8
- Song of Solomon 1:12
- Song of Solomon 2:13
- Song of Solomon 4:10-11
- Song of Solomon 7:8
- Song of Solomon 7:13
- Ezekiel 20:41
- Daniel 3:27
- Hosea 14:6
- John 12:3
- 2 Corinthians 2:15-16
- Ephesians 5:1-2
- Philippians 4:18

3
How Smell Affects our Lives

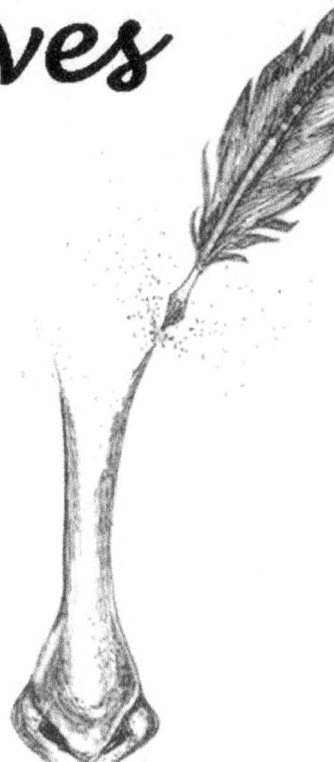

St. Paul

"Now thanks be unto God, which always causeth us to triumph in Christ, and maketh manifest the savour of his knowledge by us in every place. For we are unto God a sweet savour of Christ, in them that are saved, and in them that perish: To the one we are the savour of death unto death; to the other the savour of life unto life"
(2 Corinthians 2:14-16, KJV).

Perfume

The art of making perfume dates back to the Egyptians who used fragrances and spices quite liberally for pleasure as well as for burial and religious occasions. Sandalwood, cardamom, myrrh, cinnamon, and frankincense include some of the important scents and spices that have been traded throughout the world, throughout history. As the perfume industry developed in more modern times, fragrances were used to scent gloves, handkerchiefs, hats, and clothes while experienced and trained "noses" or experts made perfumes for the body. The ingredients of perfumes can come from flowers (geranium, rose, jasmine, orange flower, and ylang ylang) or spices and herbs (coriander, mint, black pepper, cardamom, and citrus products). Today, synthetic fragrances, typically dissolved in alcohol, have replaced the natural, more expensive fragrances. Synthetic, cheaper fragrances can be strong in their initial impact but shorter-lived in their effects.

Perfumes contain mixes of chemicals that volatilize at different rates, creating a blend of scents that fade with distance and with time at different rates, creating a changing aroma. We all vary in our sensitivities to a perfume's mix of volatile chemicals. We also vary in how we apply perfume. Elderly women who lose their sense of smell tend to over apply their perfume. On the other hand, young men tend to apply too much cologne. A good fragrance properly applied creates tension, teases the nose, soothes the senses, invigorates the body, and arouses the emotions.

> **EXAMPLE**
>
> *Every morning I sense her entry into her adjoining cubicle – long before I hear her talking on the phone. Her unique citrusy, earthy scent irritates my olfactory organ. I toyed with the idea of starting my own coffee club so the aroma of brewed coffee might drown out her perfume. But then, I worried, she might apply it in even stronger dosages.*

Perfume scents are complex and quite varied. They range from earthy, woody, balsamic to spicy, floral, fruity and citrusy, to herbal, green, minty, and to oceany and musky. The chemical odors of a perfume are said to appear in "chords" or groups of odors like the way musical notes build to form a musical chord. A perfume's fragrance can be experienced as a "composition" similar to music or a painting: with balance, feeling, energy, and character. These aspects of a perfume's fragrance are separated into the top, middle and bottom notes.

Top or head notes – These light and fleeting first impressions might include cedarwood, cypress, galbanum, ginger, citrus, orange, and mint.

Middle or heart notes – These scents are the background fragrance or blend of the perfume. Examples include basil, clove, cinnamon, jasmine, pepper, floral, violet, lily, lilac, citrus, lavender, and rose. It is interesting to note that the same flowers grown in different soils or different regions of the world will develop variations of the flower's smell – for example, roses from different countries smell different.

Base or dry-out notes – These heavy, lasting fragrances of the perfume persist when the top and middle notes fade away. These come from such fragrances as frankincense, myrrh, and sandalwood. The odors might be musky, woody, vanilla, earthy, musty, green, piney, or balsamic. Civet and musk, at low levels, provide persistence to perfumes. Cheap, synthetic perfumes can have disagreeable base notes.

> **EXAMPLE**
>
> *I knew she was not a sophisticated woman. I detected cheap perfume on the dress she left strewn across the sofa, and on her gloves. The characteristic fragrance (perhaps of rose) had long dissipated, and a solventy, piney base note penetrated my nostrils and turned my stomach.*

Did you ever notice the aroma of a man's cologne or a woman's perfume as they passed you by on the street? How long did the fragrance persist? What odors did you smell as they moved past? Did the aroma change with distance? Was the aroma overpowering or was it a tease to your senses?

> **EXAMPLE**
>
> *The perfume smelled differently on his wife's neck than what he remembered from the department store where the young, thin, bubbly saleswoman sprayed it onto a thin piece of paper that she waved in the air for them to smell.*

It can be difficult to evaluate a perfume in a department store – there are just too many lingering scents in the air and freshly sprayed samples are too strong to assess. Yet it's important to "try on" a perfume before you buy it. A perfume must fit your particular body chemistry at the spot of the body where it is applied (arm, neck, chest). Body oils, sweaty skin, and hair can alter its expression.

Perfumes and spices were well used in the ancient civilizations of Egypt, Greece, Persia, and the Roman Empire. Fragrant oils were used for skin care and protection. Everyday people had perfume and oil to offset body odors, for skin care, for the preparation of bodies for burial, and for the anointing of important guests.

In 1 Samuel 8:10-13 we read about daughters becoming perfumers such that the king might even take the young women for this purpose. The art of perfuming (in Samuel) was acquired during the years of captivity in Egypt. By the time of Moses, priests had become the official perfumers and their formulas were kept secret. Proverbs 27:9 tells us that ointment and perfume can make the heart feel happy. But as impurities spoil a good perfume (Eccl. 10:1), the Word of God is to be unmixed with worldly wisdom.

> Write an Outline to Practice Speaking on *A Holy Fragrance* using the following Bible verses:
>
> - 1 Samuel 8:10-13
> - Proverbs 27:9
> - Ecclesiastes 10:1

King Solomon had a mountain of myrrh and a hill of frankincense (Song of Solomon 4:6) and many other fragrant materials grown in his gardens. There were fig trees (2:13); pomegranates (4:13 and 6:11); flowers (5:13) and beds of spices (6:2); apples or apricots (2:3); camphire and spikenard (1:14); cedar trees (1:17); mandrakes (7:13) and lilies (4:5); balsam trees oozing out myrrh (1:13) and all chief spices (4:14). Solomon described the very name of God as ointment poured forth such as with frankincense, myrrh, saffron, camphire, pomegranates, aloes, cinnamon, and calamus.

An ointment is a highly viscous substance used on skin as a cosmetic or salve. The word ointment could be rendered anointing oil (Eccl. 7:1). God gave Moses instructions for making an ointment – a base of olive berry oil to which was added fine powders such as frankincense and myrrh. Pomade is a perfumed ointment often used to groom the hair. The process for preparation of pomade is called enfleurage wherein a fragrance is transferred from flowers or other substances to another absorbent. Highly refined lard or tallow, for example, is molded into a slab to absorb the fragrances. Freshly picked flowers, with all impurities removed, are placed between the slabs to allow the fragrances to be absorbed. Pomade de jasmin is made from jasmine flowers. A broader application of this is found in Esther 2:12-13, where the women spent a full year in preparation for the day they would be presented to the king. Their bodies became living pomades.

EXERCISE

To research the sensory aspects of perfume for a story, gather samples from the beauty section of the department store. For each perfume you want to study, bring two cotton balls in a plastic bag, tucked inside a second plastic bag, with labels you can fill out by the name of the perfume. Spray the cotton balls with the perfume's sample bottle and close off the bags. Back at home, smell the top notes first, with short sniffs. Then breathe some fresh air before smelling the heart notes. Once the perfume dissipates for a few hours or a day, check out the base notes. You should be able to pick out three to six fragrances in the blend of each perfume.

Emotion-evoking Aromas

Emotions can be brought on by odors because they induce memory. One odor may remind you of your grandmother's house, while another may smell like a baseball mitt. We associate odors with experiences – smells like an onion, smells like ammonia cleaner, smells like a burnt match. Whether or not you believe that fragrances have therapeutic effects, they do instigate memory and emotion.

The link between odors and health dates back in history. At one time people carried around pomanders or bags containing a mixture of aromatic substances to protect them from poisonous vapors. The significance of fragrances was built into everyday life through folk-lore, songs, and medicine.

EXAMPLE

The long, hot shower soothed my body as well as my mind. The rose-scented body soap and the floral lavender shampoo brought a sense of healing to my soul. I didn't want to ever leave the shower and face life again.

"**Aromatherapy**" came from the French chemist Rene Gattefosse who, during the 1930s, developed the use of aromatics for human benefit. Aromatherapy makes use of essential oils from natural roots, seeds, leaves, flowers, herbs, fruit and wood to affect physical and psychological health in positive ways. The effects can be different for men versus women. Rose oils have been suggested for constipation, depression, headaches, insomnia, nausea and nervousness. Rose petals used in bath water have been suggested for rheumatism. Orange, rose, and lavender oils improve mental function or mental relaxation. High blood pressure might be alleviated with garlic or hyssop oils. Depression and anxiety might be relieved by the aromas lavender, chamomile, frankincense, geranium, ginger, jasmine, sandalwood, peppermint and rose. A stimulating aroma might come from lime, lemon, jasmine or pine. Sleep might be encouraged with lavender, rose or sandalwood scented oils.

EXAMPLE

He learned how to demonstrate his love for her. Though exhausted after a day's work, he would sit on the throw rug and rub her aching heals with the oil of her favorite fragrance. She would close her eyes and a gentle smile would spread across her peaceful face.

Volatile aromatic oils are released into the air, whereas fatty oils are applied to the skin. These fragrances can be inhaled or absorbed through the skin during massage, body wraps, compresses, facials, and baths. The inhalation of a fragrance can be detected in one's blood stream at its peak level in minutes to an hour after initial exposure. Their presence in blood alters the body depending on where it is absorbed, how it is distributed throughout the body, and how quickly it is eliminated from the body. The application of oils during massaging can have combined effects; gentle stroking stimulates the body to release oxytocin, which dampens the hormones produced when you are stressed.

EXAMPLE

She lit a candle – one of those large, colored, scented ones. The smell of apple spice filled the air. It reminded me of my mother's room – the place I ran to and hid when dad came home drunk. While it induced romance in her, the memory it evoked for me killed the mood.

Aromatherapy catalogs can be found on the Internet or ordered. These catalogs list oils and candles and other scented products for producing various beneficial effects. You can examine labels on tea bags and candles – they provide suggestions as to how fragrances might influence mood. Some make claims of health benefits, which you can use in your story without suggesting that they actually work.

However, people can be easily influenced to feel positive or negative effects from aromas. By suggesting that a certain oil will relax you, or invigorate you, you might feel relaxed irrespective of whether the aromatic oil actually had any effects on your body. The context or setting is important in this way. A candle lit room with soft music encourages the feeling or expectation of relaxation. On the other hand, people can also be influenced to find aromas annoying, even sickening. It's all in the power of suggestion.

YOUR TURN

Finish the scene:

Ah – his hands pressed deep into my back, running along my spine. It hurt so good! The sound of running water over rocks added a soothing dimension. The room was dimly lit by candles. I heard him open a bottle of oil and splash his hands. I was overcome with the aroma of . . .

The Smell of Death, Disease, and Sin

There are, generally, two types or classes of natural odors produced during decay: odors produced under aerobic or oxygen-rich conditions, and those produced under anaerobic or oxygen-deficient conditions. Aerobic odors are usually not big problems: earthy, musty, moldy, green vegetation, grassy. Anaerobic odors are usually the problem. They give rise to the stink of marshes, drains, sewage, and infected pus. If you take a cutting of grass and place it in water, it will decay. The water will smell grassy at first. But this will change to a hay-like odor, and then to a decaying vegetation smell. After days of decay, it will turn septic and become rotten smelling. While decay is a natural process, the odors that arise from it can be quite obnoxious.

All living things are composed of proteins and amino acids. When living things decay, microorganisms decompose the proteins and amino acids to make sulfury odors such as the smell of rotten eggs or hydrogen sulfide. Other sulfury odors are septic, rotten cabbage, decaying vegetation, skunky and marshy. Amino acids and proteins also contain nitrogen, which microorganisms use to produce nitrogenous odors such as dead crab, cadaverous, and fishy.

EXAMPLE

The house had been empty for months. The trap in the kitchen sink was dry. The decaying, sulfury odors from the septic system rose out of the drain pipes, filling the room with the stink like an outhouse that needed emptying. I turned on the tap to let water run all night to flush out the system.

The smell of anaerobic decay is often associated with death, while the smell of aerobic decay is often associated with fermentation or moldiness. When a bottle of wine goes bad you don't say it has died – you say it has gone moldy. When a road-kill stinks after being in the hot sun all day, you don't say the animal has fermented – you say it's a dead animal in the middle of the road. Some descriptions for the smell of decay might include: cadaverous, putrid, rancid, dead fish, dead crab, sulfurous, fishy, decaying vegetation, sewery, oniony, garlicky, skunky, eggy, rotten eggs, septic, and marshy.

We all have a unique fingerprint smell (which your pet dog or cat can recognize) that is affected by age, sex, diet, genetics, health, medication, and disease. Hair contains fats that absorb odors, thus, hairy people tend to be more odorous. Normal perspiration is nearly odorless. Body odors are produced by skin bacteria that decompose fatty secretions from apocrine glands which are found in the armpits. Your body's odor changes with fear, stress, and excitement. Bad breath is also produced by bacteria in your mouth. A dry mouth will produce stronger odors.

> ### EXAMPLE
>
> *The compost gave off a sickening odor – one of rotting animal. The smell traveled a mile down the road. The local farmers asked the sheriff to check it out because good compost has an earthy, moldy, hay-like odor. This was not normal mulch – there was something horrible hidden in that pile.*

Human smells have assisted doctors over time in diagnosing diseases. For example, you would give off the smell of baked bread if you had typhoid fever. Yellow fever smells like a butcher's shop; smallpox like geese. A wound infection might smell like a musty wine cellar. Diabetes would give your breath a smell like apples, whereas arsenic poisoning would give your breath a smell like garlic.

The smell of death is well known by people who handle dead human bodies. Two chemicals particularly stand out for their nauseating odors. Cadaverine, associated with the smell of human corpses, is very foul-smelling and is produced by the action of bacteria on nitrogen-based proteins. Decaying fish can also have this odor. If you come in contact with it, your clothes will smell foul for days afterwards. However, you can buy cadaverine in hunting supply stores to attract coyotes, fox, and other scavengers. It is sometimes used to train search and rescue dogs. Putrescine is another obnoxious chemical, similar to cadaverine in many ways. Both contribute to the smell of decaying flesh, but also make up the smell of bad breath.

Police officers and coroners have come up with tricks to block the nauseating smell of death. They rub Vaseline under their noses to absorb the odors or smoke cigars to mask the nauseating odors of death. However, when a person dies his body does not give off such bad odors overnight. It could take several days depending on the reason for death and the temperature of the place where the body lies. The smell, over a period of a week or more, might change from no particular smell to a smell like natural gas, to the terrible smell of decay, to an ammonia-like odor, and back to barely noticeable.

The smell or taste of blood is often described as metallic in character. This smell is a result of the iron in the blood and its reactions with our skin and nasal membranes.

The Bible, directly and indirectly, mentions unpleasant odors. Ecclesiastes 10:1 tells us that dead flies spoil a perfume and make it stink. Beelzebub was the lord of the flies for the Philistines – their land was infested with annoying flies. The Jews used this name to mean the god of dung or god of the unclean. In Nehemiah 2:13 we read that one of the gates at Jerusalem was the dung gate or the place where the waste of the city was expelled. This was not the gate through which you would want to enter the city!

Sin is associated with bad smells. In Jonah 4 we find that a worm got in the gourd of the vine and it withered. The sun beat down on the decaying gourd, which developed a vile odor such that Jonah became faint from the sun and the odor. To God, we are a stench unto death as we exist in an unsaved condition. We are a stench that is unbearable to be around. In Daniel 3 we read about Shadrach, Meshach, and Abednego re-emerging from the very hot furnace of King Nebuchadnezzar, and their hair was not singed, nor their clothes charred – and they did not even smell of smoke and fire. The Lord protected them with His holiness such that there was no sin to burn off.

> Write an Outline to Practice Speaking on *That Stinking Sin* using the following Bible verses:
>
> - Proverbs 5:3-4
> - Lamentations 3:15
> - Lamentations 3:19
> - Amos 4:10
> - Amos 5:7
> - Revelation 8:10-11

Wormwood is a name for a shrubby plant that flowers during late summer and yields a bitter extract. It has a strong minty, spicy, and aromatic odor. People thought it had magic powers. It was considered poisonous enough to keep moths away. It is associated with decay, judgment, and death. In Deuteronomy 29:18 we read that we should make sure there is no wormwood within our gathering, because it is a bitter poison. Poisonous drink and food was bitter (Jer. 9:15 and 23:15). A curse or bitter judgment in Revelation is associated with wormwood (Rev. 8:10-11).

One thing is sure, without Christ to save us, we are all destined for a sensory nightmare. The ears will hear weeping and gnashing of teeth in Gehenna, Hell, the Lake of Fire, the Lake of Burning Sulfur. The smell of Hell will be most horrible – with putrid smells of sulfur and burning flesh. Even a bad taste in the mouth will appear when exposed to the overwhelmingly bad odors. The visual experience will be violent, frightening, and most ugly. The skin, or largest sensory organ of the body, will overload the brain with pain (Rev. 16:10-11). The response to Hell will be screaming, choking, uncontrollable shaking, a clawing out of the eyes, and a puncturing of the ear drums.

Yet the message of Christ is salvation from this sensory hell. Martha warned Jesus to not remove the stone to Lazarus' tomb (John 11:38-40) because Lazarus had been dead long enough to begin to stink. The smell of the decaying body would have been sickening. But Jesus called Lazarus out, to take off his rags of death and decay and to put on the fragrance of new life. And the same is true for us – Christ experienced death (Heb. 2:9) so that we could become a pleasing aroma to God.

YOUR TURN

Finish the scene:

We lived were we could afford to live. The trailer park was surrounded by swamp. The road was clay and gravel. And when the wind blew from the southeast, the smell of . . .

The Anointed One

To be anointed is to be consecrated and set aside for service to the king or to our Lord. Holy anointing oil was the final product of the perfumer (Ex. 30:22-25 and 37:29). A priest, prophet, or king (Ex. 30:30) or an object (the temple) could be anointed (Ex. 30:25-29). Moses anointed the tabernacle and all its furnishings. The same process was used whether anointing one's body for decoration or for preservation after death. In Isaiah 61:1-7 and Psalm 45:7 we read about the oil of gladness – oil that penetrates deep into the heart and carries the fragrance of blessings. Whereas in the Old Testament, anointing was done with oil; in the New Testament we are anointed with the Holy Spirit and made righteous for service to the Lord, taking on the fragrance of Christ. Anointing oil is one representation of the Holy Spirit (Ps. 89:20). In 1 Samuel 16:12-13, Samuel anointed David using the horn of oil, and David became filled with the Spirit. In Acts 10:38 we read that God anointed Jesus with the Holy Spirit. Jesus is *The Anointed One*, the *Christ*.

The Bible describes some of the formulas for oils, ointments, and incense (Ex. 30:22-25). The incense for the altar and the anointing oils used by priests had to be made in specific ways (Ex. 30:31-33). Not only the equipment but the methodology was to follow God's standards. For example, perfumers were forbidden to crush the spices under the wheel of a cart or use a staff to beat cumin (Isa. 28:27). A rod of just the right shape and weight had to be used to beat the materials into a powder. The oil base had to be oil of olive. The proportioning of ingredients had to be exact.

The first mention in the Bible of anointing is in Genesis 28:18. Here Jacob had left his home. Sand became his bed and a stone became his pillow. Taking the stone, he anointed it with oil as an altar to the Lord. Jacob used olive oil. Olive oil was carried for minor injuries and for protection against the hot sun as well as for other purposes (Ex. 27:20). Pure olive oil was also important in the Hebrew diet (Num. 11:7-8). Perhaps he blended it with other scents before anointing the stone.

There are over 200 references to olive oil in the Bible, showing its many uses. It was obtained from the best ripened olives – beaten and strained through finely woven baskets, and settled (the oil was decanted off the top). Animal or fish oils were not acceptable. Oil from the ground was not acceptable. Gethsemane was the place where olives grew and were pressed under heavy weight to bring out the valuable olive oil. Gethsemane is also where Jesus was heavily pressed and sweated blood in prayer before God, His Father.

Purified nard, or spikenard, was carried in an alabaster flask, vial, or jar. Spikenard comes from the root of an aromatic herb and was saved for special occasions. In Mark 14:3 we find a woman with an alabaster box of spikenard. She broke the box and poured the ointment on the Lord as a sign that she owned him as her Lord. In Matthew 26 and Mark 14, Mary was said to have poured the liquid perfume or ointment on Jesus' head. In John 12 Jesus was anointed on his feet, and then not wasting any of the precious oil the woman let her hair down to wipe up the rest with her hair. Her hair then carried the same precious scent that Jesus had (she identified herself with Jesus). It was proper for a host to wash the feet of a special guest, so the feet washing was not unusual (and perhaps this was why Mark and Matthew focused on the unusual anointment of Jesus' head, as well as on the use of expensive, purified spikenard).

Jesus likely went to His death still smelling of the aromatic oil or perfume that Mary had lavishly poured upon him. Jesus commented that the perfume was good to use while He was yet alive (Matt. 26:12). It was not the religious officials who anointed Jesus, but a sinner out of humble sacrifice, using a very expensive perfume that she had saved in an ornate alabaster jar for her own burial. Mary did not realize the fullness of the symbolism of this act for the life of Jesus. Perhaps, though, she did somewhat comprehend who He was and more importantly, the great thanks to be given Him after He raised Lazarus from the dead.

A balm is a Mediterranean herb of the mint family. It can have a lemon scent to its leaves and would be used in teas. Other balms come from aromatic resins of trees and shrubs and are used as a salve or oil for comfort and healing. Anointing of sick people was a medicinal technique done by rubbing rather than by pouring oil. Egyptians used essential oils during massage treatments, a technique that today is called aromatherapy.

> Write an Outline to Practice Speaking on *God's Anointed* using the following Bible verses:
>
> - Exodus 29:7
> - Exodus 29:21
> - Exodus 30:22-29
> - Exodus 40:9
> - Leviticus 16:32
> - Deuteronomy 28:40
> - 1 Samuel 16:13
> - 2 Samuel 14:2
> - Psalm 45:7
> - Matthew 6:16-17
> - Mark 6:13
> - Mark 14:3-8
> - Luke 7:44-47
> - John 12:3
> - Acts 10:38
> - 1 John 2:27

The balm of Gilead (Jer. 8:22) is from a tree or shrub of Arabia and Somalia that has heart-shaped leaves and provided good shade. The balm of Gilead is mentioned in Genesis and Jeremiah. It is interesting that Gilead was referred to as a refuge to flee from one's enemy (1 Sam. 13:7; Gen. 29-31). Hippocrates, the Father of Medicine, reportedly freed Athens from the pestilence by burning the fragrant plant in the city's streets.

Environmental Fragrancing

Environmental fragrancing is the controlled dispensing of fragrances into specific settings to enhance mood. For example, an eye-opening citrus scent would help you wake up in the morning, but at noon you might want a calming floral scent, followed by a soothing woodland in the evening. Lime or lemon aroma might help you focus on work. Lavender and peppermint might improve work efficiency. Jasmine and pine might add a stimulating sensation to enhance energy levels. A pine forest smell can be invigorating – as a walk outdoors on a cool morning.

> EXAMPLE
>
> *As she moved from compartment to compartment, the lighting and color accommodated her mood – soft jazz music played in the background as the air vents puffed out a soothing eucalyptus scent. The space station sensed her needs better than she knew them herself.*

There are consultants and companies that provide fragrances and technologies to disperse the fragrances for businesses, hotels, hospitals, and prisons. A sports department might dispense the scent of leather baseball mitt; the baby section of baby powder; the customer complaint desk of calming sandalwood. Hotel rooms might be fragranced with a soothing lavender aroma. **Fragrances have become as common as Muzak** in stores where the amount of time you browse can be influenced by the environmental fragrances. Fragrances can even be part of the branding or marketing of a product such as a cell phone or laptop computer. You are familiar with the "new car" smell. There are even scents that provide a paper book smell (for those who switched to eBooks). Devices can emit scents such as when specific songs are played, a phone rings, or when the morning alarm clock wakes you up.

> **EXAMPLE**
>
> *At midnight, the clock in the hallway chimed – the floodlights outside the house extinguished – the fragrance of the room changed from a piney invigorating scent to a sleepy lavender aroma. The house and its inhabitants drifted off to a deep and peaceful sleep.*

The human chemical that helps to regulate your cycles of sleep and wake is **melatonin** – a hormone secreted by the pineal gland. It can be taken in small doses to control the sleep cycle. There are essential oils that provide an alternative to taking this hormone.

> **EXAMPLE**
>
> *The detective picked up the wool jacket and sniffed at its sleeves and collar: "So, you said, you have just come from the gym and your secretary was at the spa? Would you say that the gym's locker room smells like rosemary? Is there something else you want to tell me?"*

There are, on the other hand, people who cannot tolerate anything but scent-free air and they need to avoid irritating chemicals in perfumes and other scented products. Malodors have been known to impair work performance and health, and make people feel sick.

YOUR TURN

Finish the scene:

I was blindfolded, but I could still smell. The car door opened and they pushed and pulled me out. The smell of garbage dumpster, moldy brick, and car exhaust whiffed through my nasal passageway. A heavy steel door opened and I was ushered inside, where I could smell . . .

Incense is Something Burned

Incense comes from aromatic substances, such as from a wood or gum, and is burned to release fragrant odors. Incense is something that must be set on fire and burned. In 2 Chronicles 2:4, Solomon talks about burning incense in the name of the Lord. Without fire there is no fragrance. Fire is essential for releasing the pleasing aroma of incense. The word "aroma" comes from the Greek "airo" for "lift up" (to take up and away). Fire is a symbol of purifying, as to come forth as pure gold or to go through trial by fire. In Daniel 3 we find three men who were put into the fire. God did not put out the fire; He stepped into the fire to be with them (perhaps we too must pass through fiery trials to release our sweetest fragrance).

In Egypt, incense played a part in religious rites such as burial ceremonies. The Book of the Dead documents Egyptians using prayers and the burning of incense to help the dead resist corruption from evil spirits in the darkness, to pass into the next life, and to unite with their gods. The burning of incense to please gods is still widespread. In Japan, such a practice still exists at Buddhist temples. People write prayers or petitions on sticks of pine. These are then given to the Buddhist priests. The priests pray and put the sticks in fires to burn so that the petitions ascend into the spiritual realm along with the pleasing aroma of pine and incense.

In the Bible, incense was burned at the burial of kings in the belief that the pleasing aroma ascended to the nostrils of the god(s), preparing the way for the king and for his acceptance (Jer. 34:5; 2 Chron. 21:18-19). In Ezra 6:9-10 these practices made sure that prayers for the king and his family were acceptable to God. A similar practice can be found in Job 1:5. Burning incense was also done to idols (Jer. 11:12). Incense is representative of continuous praise and prayer (Ex. 30:7-8; Mal. 1:11). As Aaron offered incense for Israel, so the Lord prays for his own people (John 17:9). As Aaron entered into the holy place to burn incense, Christ entered heaven and offers up appeasement to the Father for His people. Incense symbolizes the prayers of intercession of Christ on our behalf (Rom. 8:34; Heb. 7:25). It was offered as an intercession to the High Priest (Rev. 8: 3-4) and so we are to offer up continual sacrifices pleasing to God (Heb. 13:15-16).

The temple had an altar for the burning of incense (Ex. 37:25-29). In Numbers 29:1-6 we read that these were offerings of pleasing aromas made to the Lord by fire. Offerings that were burned turned into smoke and sparks that ascended upwards toward heaven. Thus the burnt offering was wholly burnt. Blood was sprinkled on the object before it was burned. This symbolically foreshadowed the offering of Christ, at the great altar of Jerusalem, where Christ was sacrificed and then ascended to heaven to gain our acceptance by God.

In the Old Testament the burnt offering and the grain offering involved incense (Lev. 2:1-3). Oil and frankincense accompanied the meat offering. However, the sin offering was different – it did not use oil or incense on it, because it was a sin offering (Lev. 5:11-13). Christ was a sin offering (obtaining pardon on our behalf) as His blood flowed down from the cross. In a sin offering the blood was poured down the side of the altar, the animal was burned on the ground, and the odor was not a sweet savor. God gave very specific directions on preparing the offerings. The directions had to be followed – there would be serious punishment if they were not followed to the detail.

Incense was an important part of ceremonies where honor or tribute was to be paid in life and in death (2 Chron. 16:13-14; Dan. 2:46-47). In Numbers 7 we read about the dedication of the altar wherein one prince from every tribe of Israel presented offerings to Aaron along with incense (enough for a day) because Aaron went in to the altar carrying only as much as was needed for each day (Lev. 16:12). The incense of the Old Testament temple was a mixture of spices (Ex. 30:34-35). The blending was critical. Some of the ingredients of incense include a hardened gum that oozed out of cuts in the storax tree like raindrops. This tree grew abundantly in Galilee.

Another ingredient was **onycha** – probably the operculum of a mollusc found in the Holy Land. A small horny shield on the mollusc foot gives off an odor. Although the musky odor is not in itself agreeable, it enhances other odorous substances – a typical function of musky-type odors.

Galbanum is a pine or green-like odor that enhances other odors and was likely added to incense. It comes from a common perennial weed in the carrot family that grows up to several feet high in Syria and Persia. A stinky yellowish-brown gum oozes from cuts in the weed and hardens. It has a sharp bitter taste.

A very common ingredient of incense was and still is **frankincense**. It is mentioned throughout the Bible. "Frank" means free, or that it was inexpensive and readily available. It readily ignites, burning with a white flame, giving off a pleasant balsamic odor.

Write an Outline to Practice Speaking on *Incensed about the Bible* using the following Bible verses:

- Exodus 30:1
- Exodus 30:34-38
- Exodus 40:5
- Leviticus 4:7
- Leviticus 10:1-2
- Numbers 16:46
- 2 Chronicles 26:16-19
- Psalm 141:2
- Ezekiel 8:11
- Malachi 1:11
- Luke 1:8-11
- Revelation 8:3-4

Incense is given up with prayers, or the prayers of the saints are like incense (Ps. 141:2; Rev. 5:8 and 8:3-4). But there are times when our sin cannot be masked by incense. Incense and perfume were expensive and therefore kept in expensive alabaster jars with tight seals. In contrast, God places in us the fragrance of Christ, the gospel news – yet we are clay pots that crack and leak. Incense is often burned in covered vessels or censers, used to safely dispense the fragrance. We are to be like censers (2 Cor. 2:14) spreading the fragrance of the knowledge of Christ – the gospel.

Clothing and Building Materials

A man who follows in Christ's footsteps can be said to have upon him a fragrant covering (Ps. 45:7-8). The aroma that comes from an excellent man is wonderful. Now when you bring such men together in unity you have a fragrant gathering (Ps. 133:1-2).

Aaron, as a high priest, had garments that smelled of myrrh and aloes in addition to the odor of anointing oil (Ex. 29:21). In Genesis 49:11, clothes were washed in wine perhaps to foreshadow the Last Supper of Christ. Psalm 45:7-8 recorded a song of praise for the king wherein there was an anointing of robes with myrrh, aloes, and cassia.

In the story of Esau and Jacob (Gen. 27), Esau was a man of the field and the earth was his bed. His clothing smelled of plowed earth. Jacob who was Rebekah's favorite stayed home. **Rebekah had to make Jacob smell like Esau to obtain his father's blessing, and so she used Esau's clothing.** It is interesting to note that the field was likened to the world by its earthy smell. As we associate with the world we absorb its odors: we take on a worldly smell. With this smell we have no inheritance from the Father.

The Bible recorded the use of cedar wood (2 Sam. 7:1-2). Cedar fagots would be cast into the fire at the altar to add to the fragrance that was released. Cedars have durable, aromatic and insect resistant wood. Cedar wood represents something with preservative properties against mold and decay. Cedar gives off a strong but pleasant odor. Not only is cedar an excellent wood but it can fill a building with its fragrance.

The majestic cedars of Lebanon were used for the temple. The cedar of Lebanon is a large cedar native to Lebanon and Turkey. The cedar's foliage gives off a pungent aromatic odor when crushed. Cedar represented strength and lasting qualities (Hosea 14:5-6).

An Egyptian embalming ritual involved rubbing the skin of the deceased with cedar oil and myrrh. The body would be stuffed with particles of aromatic woods and linen cloth was used as wrap saturated with fragrant perfume. Recall the burial of Jesus – Nicodemus brought a mixture of myrrh and aloes and wrapped Him up with the spices, in strips of fragrant linen, according to Jewish burial custom (John 19:38-40).

Aloe wood was also used. Aloe comes from the tree after it is cut down. This wood has a soft resinous quality and was desirable for perfumes. The wood was sometimes buried for a time to hasten its decay so that when it was burned it would give off a fuller aroma. Aloe is obtained from the core of a cut tree. There is a popular belief that the tree from which aloe perfume is obtained is the only tree descended from the Garden of Eden and is therefore called the Paradise Tree.

The tabernacle was built using shittim wood and some of it was overlaid with gold, over which was anointing oil. Gold represented royalty as on a kingly crown. Shittim or acacia (Ex. 36: 20,31) is a fragrant wood that was used to make parts of the ark of the covenant, the altar, and the tabernacle. The materials of the tabernacle were then anointed to make them holy (Ex. 40:9).

Write an Outline to Practice Speaking on *The Bible's Instruction for Construction* using the following Bible verses:

- Genesis 49:11
- 2 Samuel 7:1-3
- Psalm 45:7-8
- Psalm 133:1-2
- Song of Solomon 4:11
- John 19:38-40

4
Describing Beverages, Spices, and Fish

Ray Bradbury –
The Martian Chronicles

Now it was as if a great wind has washed the land clean of sounds. There was nothing. Skeleton doors hung open on leather hinges. Rubber-tire swings hung in the silent air, uninhibited. The washing rocks at the river were empty, and the watermelon patches, if any, were left alone to heat their hidden liquors in the sun. Spiders started building new webs in abandoned huts; dust started to sift in from unpatched roofs in golden spicules. Here and there a fire, forgotten in the last rush, lingered and in a sudden access of strength fed upon the dry bones of some littered shack. The sound of a gentle feeding burn went up through the silenced air.
  (New York: Bantam, 1975), 96

A Sip of Water

Why do so many people drink **bottled water**? One reason, so they claim, is that bottled water tastes better than tap water. Most public tap waters in North America have chlorine in the water which gives the water a chlorinous flavor. Others say they drink bottled water because they are accustomed to a certain taste. While some people grew up on well water, others grew up on public tap water, and others perhaps drank too little water to know the difference. However, there are some tap waters that taste good enough to be bottled, there are bottled waters that need more treatment, and there are cool, clear well waters that are contaminated with dangerous chemicals. Finally, water can be overly purified such that the natural minerals giving it a refreshing taste have been removed, leaving the water flat tasting.

Fine restaurants do not serve tap water as the "house water," but serve bottled water – perhaps even with a wedge of lemon in it. You may prefer not to have ice in your water, especially if the water is bottled water. Bad ice can ruin good water. Some restaurants offer a choice of mineral water, sparkling water, or spring water. Such bottled waters can range in price from a few dollars a bottle to 10s of dollars a bottle, and have quite elaborate bottle shapes, colors, and labeling. Bottled waters can be domestic or they can be imported from all around the world: South America, Europe, Scandinavia, Asia, Australia, New Zealand, Fiji, and so forth. A restaurant might even have a "water bar" where you can taste dozens of different waters. Just as choosing the right wine for a dinner, different courses (appetizer, main course, and desert) can have different waters as guided by the restaurant's sommelier or trained taste expert. They may even serve different waters in different glasses – from short goblets to tall, thin glasses.

When you describe the **flavor of water** as "refreshing and pure" or "objectionable" you are not using true sensory descriptions, but rather emotional responses and judgments. The following is a summary of the taste and smell qualities of various waters to help you provide added flavor to your description:

Cold tap water from a public water supply will have a chlorinous, bleachy, swimming pool flavor from the chlorine, usually at a level that is slight or barely noticeable. A musty or earthy odor can come from the water source; a metallic, rusty aftertaste can come from corroding pipes, or there may be a plastic flavor if new plastic plumbing has been installed.

Hot tap water can smell sulfurous, oily, or hydrocarbon-like from the hot water pipes and heating system. Heating tap water enhances the release of water odors, making these odors more noticeable. Hot water can have a musty smell.

Spring water is expected to be tasteless and odorless, but can also be astringent or impart a drying sensation or a flat taste depending on the levels of minerals.

Well water is expected to be tasteless and odorless. A rusty, metallic aftertaste or sulfurous odor can come from iron- and sulfur-bearing well waters. A salty taste lingers if dissolved minerals are too high or salt water has intruded into the well. Some groundwater supplies are contaminated with a sweet, chemical, solvent-like odor from industrial chemicals.

Bottled water is expected to be tasteless and odorless, but it can be flat-tasting if the minerals are too low, as with purified bottled water. A sweet taste or a plastic flavor can come from the plastic bottle, especially under poor storage conditions (when the bottle has been sitting in direct sunlight). A chemical, gasoline, or oily smell can appear if the water has been stored in the trunks of cars allowing chemicals to permeate through the plastic bottle. Finally, there's a growing market of flavored bottled waters and vitamin-enriched waters of various flavors.

Mineral water can have a sulfurous odor, a salty, bitter, or sour taste, an astringent sensation, and a tongue-coating feeling caused by its high mineral content or dissolved solids. These waters can be "still" (non-carbonated) or sparkling (carbonated). A sparkling water can have small bubbles or large bubbles, which define its effervescence. Carbonation can be added during bottling or it can be naturally found with the water.

Ocean water has a lingering, overpowering salty taste with a mouth coating feeling.

Polluted river water odors can vary from decaying vegetation, septic, swampy, soapy, oily, earthy, fishy, medicinal, or phenolic, to chemical and a mixture of these.

Eutrophic (algae laden) lake or pond water can vary from grassy, decaying vegetation, hay-like, swampy or marshy, earthy or musty, to fishy and a mixture of these – such as with a fishy, musty, slightly grassy smell.

Consider the following example of a man, alone in the country, who needed a drink of water after he lost his supplies to a crazed grizzly bear, and was left wandering around for hours without anything to drink:

EXAMPLE

He cupped his hands, dipping into the pond's muddy water. This was not the safe water at home in his kitchen, but out here in the wild it was all he had. He drank deeply out of his hands and dipped for more.

This scene can be embellished by adding in more sensory descriptions:

EXAMPLE (rewritten)

He cupped his hands, dipping into the pond's muddy water. An odor of decaying vegetation arose. This was not safe water at home in his kitchen, but out here in the wild it was all he had. He drank deeply, not sure if the earthy flavor was from the water or from his dirty hands, and dipped for more.

In summary, here's a list of some sensory characteristics to describe various types of water:

Tastes: salty, sour, bitter.

Mouthfeel: astringent, drying, slick, tongue-coating, carbonated, soapy, acidic.

Odors: chlorinous, swimming pool, earthy, musty, swampy, marshy, fishy, grassy, decaying vegetation, rotten eggs, sulfurous, oily, septic, hay-like, medicinal, rusty, metallic.

The next time your character takes a sip of water, remember that you can add a little "flavor" to your story to help it "feel" more real for your readers.

EXERCISE

Go to the grocery store and buy different brands of bottled water. Buy colored cups and number the bottoms with numbers matching the bottled waters. Fill the cups half full. Allow them all to reach room temperature. Ask someone to rearrange the cups so you cannot tell which cup has which number. Now taste each cup of water and try to match it by taste to the brands. Test how discerning is your taste for water.

Coffee's Aroma

Coffee dates back to the 15th and 17th centuries in North Africa and Turkey. It found its way to the New World (North America) through Italy and England. At various times in US history, coffee has competed against beer and alcoholic beverages to be the favored drink.

> **EXAMPLE**
>
> *He said we'd meet at the town's only coffee café. It was a rainy night and there was no one to provide directions. So I followed the nutty aroma of roasted, coffee through the warm, damp air down the alleys, through the courtyard, and up to the café's front door. As the clock chimed 10, there he sat, slurping from a small cup and smiling at me.*

Coffee is consumed typically before or after a meal and should be served as soon after brewing as possible to enjoy its freshest flavor. Although coffee is simply roasted coffee beans and water, it comes in different colors and flavors with the addition of cream, sugar, milk, and powdered or non-dairy creamer. Coffee can be flavored with ground chicory root, toasted barley, dried figs, spices, vanilla, chocolate, liquors, and nuts. Coffee can have its beans spiced ahead of time or you can add syrups after brewing.

Coffee beans, or seeds of the fruit of a tropical tree, take on flavors according to the environment in which they grow. Improper handling of beans leads to off aromas. Caffeine is naturally found in the coffee bean (with chocolate, caffeine is in the cocoa bean). **Caffeine provides a bitter taste and enhances the flavor.** Beans are ground, blended or mixed (most American coffees are blended), and roasted. Roasting is largely responsible for the flavor of coffee. The lightest roast, common in the USA, is the American roast. The French and Brazilian roasts are dark. The Viennese roast is darker. The Espresso roast is the darkest, sometimes even burnt.

EXAMPLE

I ordered decaf, but an hour later I was bouncing off the walls. I should have tasted the difference. The coffee was especially bitter, and I didn't have any cream or milk to soften it. Now I know not to buy coffee from the mini-mart around the corner. As the court stenographer, I can't afford to be hyped up like this during a drawn-out trial.

There are several types of coffee beverages. **Espresso** uses roasted dark beans for a strong, rich flavor. **Cappuccino** contains espresso and an equal amount of steamed milk and foamed milk. **Caffè latte** contains a small amount of espresso with steamed milk, topped off with foamed milk. **Caffè mocha** contains espresso, steamed milk and chocolate syrup topped with foamed milk or whipped cream. **Caffè au lait** (French coffee) contains strong, dark coffee and steamed milk.

Practice tasting coffee yourself. Use the following technique. Sniff, slurp to volatilize the aroma in your mouth, swish the coffee around your mouth to contact all your nerve endings, and then swallow it. Rinse your mouth with water between different coffees. If it is a rich or full-bodied coffee it will provide lots of sensations. Tastes include sour or acidity, sweet from the sugars, and bitter. The mouthfeel of coffee is astringent, oily, rough, tangy, or pungent. Note also the aftertaste or lingering sensation. An aftertaste could be smoky, chocolate, roasted, or caramel. Coffee aromas include floral, fragrant, cinnamon, grassy, earthy, citrusy, fruity, nutty, roasted, syrupy, chocolate, buttery, piney, medicinal, peppery, smoky, and burnt. Note the fullness or flatness of the body. Is the coffee thin or heavy in overall flavor?

When roasted coffee goes stale, it develops off flavors. Poor storage conditions affect coffee's flavor. Such off flavors include stale, burnt, flat, rancid, and strong bitter. Coffee is mostly water, so bad water will also affect its flavor.

All over the world, coffee houses or shops encourage people to meet, relax, read, search the Internet, answer e-mails, and even write books.

EXAMPLE

He poured me a mug of coffee, saying that it was fresh from town, and continued explaining that he had not been to the rainforest for several months. He said that our hidden treasure was untouched, safe in its original place. As I tasted the coffee, I noticed it had a medicinal, rancid off aroma – not the fragrant, cinnamon aroma of the fresh brew from town. I began doubting his story – I imagined he had been to the treasure sooner than he was leading me to believe.

Tasseography or tasseomancy is fortune telling using coffee grounds, tea leaves, or wine sediment. The technique requires that you consume all the coffee or tea, leaving the sediment or grounds behind. Once dry, your fortune is told based on where the grounds end up (rim, sides, or bottom of the cup) and the images they display (numbers, letters, heart, flowers, animals, bridge, or road, etc.). Turkish coffee is more often used for fortune telling because it leaves plenty of grounds behind.

YOUR TURN

Finish the scene:

It was my first day on the job. My boss sent me out for coffee – but I don't drink coffee and I didn't know enough to ask her what kind she wants to drink. I pondered the menu board at the coffee shop. I had never realized there were so many different brews. I decided to . . .

The Lure of Spices

Spices have cultural, religious, and spiritual significance. In 1 Kings 10:10, a gift to Solomon from the Queen of Sheba was a gift of spices in abundance. Medical men and magicians used spices and herbs for cures and charms. Spices and fragrances were added to wine. Priests burned spiced wood along with dried leaves and flowers for their gods. In Luke 11:42 we read that the Pharisees capitalized on the people's superstitions and practices, and became wealthy in the use of spices.

The lure of spices and other treasures brought warriors to the gates of Jerusalem (2 Kings 20:12-18). The spice trade greatly affected the movement of peoples in the Holy Land. Ezekiel 27:17-22 tells us that an important part of the Old Testament economy consisted of traffic in spicery. This is because spice plants contain powerful antibacterial and antifungal chemicals. Spices provide macronutrients, improve the flavor of spoiled foods, and enhance human perspiration, which increases body cooling. The beneficial use of spice in food is associated with the enhancement of flavor and the preservation of food.

Spices, as mentioned in the Bible, can be any one of a number of aromatic vegetable products:

- **Coriander:** A chief ingredient of curry powder and mentioned in Exodus 16:31 with manna. The seeds were obtained from an annual flowering herb that gives off a spicy, aromatic, and woody aroma.
- **Cumin:** It comes from a plant in Syria and Egypt. Cumin oil is known as curry. Cumin has a spicy, green, aromatic, musty aroma.
- **Myrrh:** Myrrh is the yellowish resin of a small flowering tree. Myrrh coeur is known as vinegar. Myrrh (obtained from a living tree) and aloes (obtained from a dead tree) represent the fact that

whether by life or death, Jesus released a pleasing aroma. In Genesis 37:25 we read that myrrh was carried into Egypt. Myrrh gum was used in commerce, for healing and skin care, and to scent the garments of kings (Ps. 45:8). Its aroma is bitter, spicy, balsamic, and woody. Myrrh is mentioned many times throughout the Song of Solomon. Oil of myrrh represents our Savior, and we would use it to prepare the fragrance of the community of believers as the bride of Christ.

- **Frankincense:** It comes from the orange-brownish resin of a shrubby flowering tree found in North Africa and India. Its aroma is citrusy, balsamic, camphor-like, and woody. Myrrh and frankincense are commonly associated with the visit of the wise men to Jesus (Matt. 2:11). Frankincense (often burned) represents Christ ascending, and myrrh (typically in oils for anointing) represents Christ with us.
- **Cinnamon:** It was of high demand and hard to get. It was the delight of the kings. It was obtained from the bark and leaves of the cinnamon tree that had been beaten into a fine powder. Dried ginger grass was beaten into a powder and mixed with equal parts of cinnamon to produce a balanced fragrance. Cinnamon has antibacterial properties, and thus made a good spice for the preservation of foods.
- **Cassia:** It was a popular spice of merchants (Ez. 27:19) produced from the beaten, powdered, and dried bark of a tree. Men used it to perfume their garments.
- **Rue:** It is a shrub that is also called rosemary or "herb of grace" (an emblem of remembrance and grace since it is an evergreen.). Its aroma is piney, aromatic, and spicy.
- **Saffron:** It was a costly spice that is aromatic and bitter, and comes from a type of crocus or low growing perennial that blooms in the autumn in Persia, Greece, and Asia Minor. The flowers are collected by hand and dried for the stigmas. The germinating seed is in the stigma. As much as four thousand blossoms are needed to make just one ounce of oil. Saffron releases its odor when it is beaten.
- **Spikenard or Nard:** This oil comes from the root of a plant in the highland valleys between India and Tibet. In Mark 14:3 we read about the alabaster box poured out to anoint Jesus with nard.
- **Hyssop:** This was obtained from a flowering perennial shrub. Its aroma is woody, spicy, and camphor-like.

Write an Outline to Practice Speaking on *Spicing up Your Life the Bible's Way* using the following Bible verses:

- 1 Kings 10:10
- 1 Chronicles 9:29-30
- 2 Chronicles 16:14
- Song of Solomon 4:10
- Song of Solomon 4: 13-14
- Song of Solomon 8:14
- Isaiah 39:2
- Ezekiel 27:22
- Mark 16:1
- Luke 23:55-56
- Luke 24:1
- John 19:40

Time for Tea

In many places around the world and throughout much of history, tea has been as important as water even though tea is basically water, to which are added products from the drying and processing of leaves from the tea bush. **Basically all teas come from the same plant**, but different varietals exist because the same tea leaf grown in different environments takes on unique qualities.

The history of tea dates back to the 4th century in China. Even today, most teas come from China and India. Tea flavoring, blending, processing, and tasting became quite popular as an art by the 15th century. The Dutch brought it from Japan in the 17th century, when its use became quite fashionable. In the 17th century, the English East India Company made its wealth in the trade of tea. By the 1800s, tea had become a favorite beverage in England amongst even the working class. Since tea was brewed, it provided a natural defense against waterborne germs to the point that doctors saw a decline in dysentery, cholera, and child mortality as tea became a household drink.

All true tea is naturally caffeinated, but the levels of caffeine vary depending on how the tea is processed. Some teas are blends. Natural spices, fruits, and herbs, as well as honey, lemon, sugar, and cinnamon can be added to alter the flavor of tea.

Iced tea was created in 1904 at the St. Louis World's Fair when an Englishman iced his tea to offset the heat. Iced tea can be sweetened or unsweetened, caffeinated or non-caffeinated. Sweet tea is tea that is allowed to cool with sugar added, and is common in the southern states. Tea bags were created in New York in 1908 as a cheaper, more convenient way to store and transport tea.

> **EXAMPLE**
>
> *I had put down my tea cup on the edge of the corner table. Now there were two cups. I couldn't tell which one was mine – both teas had a light color. I tasted the one closest to me. It had an aromatic, apple-spice flavor. I knew that was not mine. My tea had a peach flavor. I was so embarrassed that I kept the wrong cup, shuffling my way into the living room before anyone would notice.*

Different teas come about by different techniques for crushing and breaking the tea leaves and buds, which release enzymes and allow oxidation to take place (the more oxidation, the blacker the tea). There are four general types of tea:

White Tea – Pale green, almost clear in color. The least common type, with the lowest caffeine content. It comes from China and India. It is made by processing tea buds without allowing oxidation to take place – without breaking or disturbing the tea buds. White tea is a specialty tea.

Green Tea – Greenish to yellow in color. This is the original tea and it comes from the Orient. This tea tastes like green leaves, grass, or spinach because minimal oxidation is maintained – the leaves are gently withered before processing. It is low in caffeine content.

Oolong Tea – Amber-like in color but variable. This tea is from China and Taiwan and varies in oxidation and taste. Oolong tea falls between green and black tea. It is commonly served in Chinese restaurants in America. It is more difficult to make because the leaves are only partially oxidized or partially bruised, which is hard to control. Thus, some are more green-like while others tend to be like black tea.

Black Tea – Reddish-brown in color. Black tea is the most common and highest in caffeine. It has been fully oxidized. The broken up leaves blacken the tea. It is from India. Earl Grey is a black tea scented with citrus oil. Other common black teas include Darjeeling, Ceylon Black, and English Breakfast. Black teas have been more popular than green teas in England and America because, being more processed and oxidized, they store longer.

Tea bags do not deliver the highest quality flavor for teas. Therefore the more expensive European and Asian teas are whole leaf teas. Green and white teas, being the least oxidized, should not be steeped or allowed to sit as long in boiling water as black tea.

EXAMPLE

She continued telling her story as she poured me a cup of tea. I was tired – hardly able to keep focused on what she was saying. The tea was a bit hot, but it tasted delightful. Its invigorating lemony flavor with a flowery burst enlivened me just enough to smile and nod as she came to a pause. I took another long sip and asked, "So what did you do next?"

The body or flavor of a tea can be flat and thin, or medium, or rich and full. Tea can come in all kinds of flavors because just about any flavor enhancer can be added to tea: cardamom, cinnamon, clove, black peppercorn, etc. Tea flavors include astringent, acidic, fruity, flowery, baked bread, berry-like, burnt, roasted, earthy, grassy, herbal, straw, malty, metallic, nutty, pine-like, pungent, smoky, spicy, stale, sweet, and tangy. Tea will become more astringent or bitter tasting, and papery or stale in flavor if it has not been stored properly.

Many teas or herbal teas are claimed to have health benefits. Green tea, especially, has been linked to better health – it contains natural antioxidants. But **herbal "teas" are not true teas** since no tea leaves are used to make them. They are made from dried flowers, fruits, and herbs such as vanilla, chamomile, peach, bergamot, lemon grass, peppermint, spearmint, rosehips, hibiscus flower, orange peel, apples, strawberry leaves, lime, lemon peel, roasted chicory, lemon verbena, jasmine, and ginger. These teas can have flavors of apple, minty, lemony, spicy, herbal, aromatic, citrusy, and licorice. Chamomile tea is a very common herbal tea.

Tea can be classified according to its quality, or the physical quality of the leaf from which it was made. Pekoe grading is one example. The ratings, though, do not necessarily predict flavor quality.

If you live close to a tea house, check and see if they provide times for tea tasting.

YOUR TURN

Finish the scene:

I came home early from work with a pounding headache. No one was home, but there were two glasses of warm tea on the kitchen counter. My spouse's favorite . . .

The Bouquet of Wine

Wine dates back a long time in the Middle East and Mediterranean regions of the world, where it was common to mix it with water. Wine once defined classes, sustained military troops, supported trade, and provided for better health.

> **EXAMPLE**
>
> *Their neighbors came over at eight for the open house, bringing with them flowers, chocolate candies, welcome cards, and wine – red and white from California, Italy, France, Chile, and Australia. Their neighbors hoped they would uncork the various wines and serve them that night. Since they stored the wine away in the cellar, everyone went home early.*

Wine is served by the glass, half-bottle, or bottle. You can purchase special wine-tasting glasses that are shaped like goblets so that when wine is poured into the glasses the aroma is captured in a headspace above the wine. If you use these glasses to taste various wines you will be amazed at the many different aromas – not necessarily aromas you might expect for wine.

Red wine includes Zinfandel, Pinot Noir, Merlot, Cabernet Sauvignon, Syrah or Shiraz, Beaujolais, and Chianti. **White wine** includes Chardonnay, Riesling, Sauvignon Blanc, Chablis, and Pinot Grigio. **Table wine**, wine served with dinner, includes white and red wines. **Sparkling wine** (containing carbonation) might be served before dinner. Many wines are produced in France, Germany, Italy, Spain, Australia, Chile, Argentina, and the USA (most typically in California, Oregon, and New York).

Wine is simply grape sugar in water (grape juice) converted by yeast to alcohol, and carbon dioxide. Wine typically has between 8 to 15 percent alcohol content. **Appertif wine** is at least 15 percent by volume in alcohol. Table wines have an alcohol content less than 14 percent. The alcohol affects the flavor – giving wine a mouth and nose feel, or tingling and burning sensations. A dry wine has its sugar converted to alcohol whereas a sweet wine has a residual of unfermented sugar. Acidic, or sour tasting wine, is more often white wine. Wine can be made from other sources of sugar such as Japanese rice wine or sake.

Taste testing wine can be fun. Open the bottle and make sure the cork was securely seated. Check the cork for a corky-moldy odor (if the bottle still uses a natural cork) which alerts you that the wine has gone bad or the moldy cork has spoiled the wine. Smell the wine for vinegar, burnt-match, sulfurous, skunky, cardboard, fishy, soapy, yeasty or rancid odors, which alert you that the wine is bad.

Let wine come to a temperature that is just right for tasting. Many red wines are young and therefore benefit from being poured into a decanter (to be oxidized) for serving. Pour your glass half full. Hold your wine glass by the stem and look at the color, checking for sediment. White wines will have a straw to yellowish or gold tint. Reds have a ruby red to brownish red or purple tint. Nonetheless, whatever color, it should be clear and not cloudy. Swirl the wine to aerate it, then stick your nose down to the glass and take short sniffs. Taste the wine (sip, swirl around your mouth, swish it in your mouth to release aromas, and swallow). Notice the sugary-sweet taste. Notice how well it seems to blend. **A mature wine, or one that has aged well, has a well-balanced flavor.**

EXAMPLE

He tilted the glass of cherry-red wine, as if inspecting it for evidence. His nose almost touched the liquid. When he tasted it, his mouth swished and munched. He closed his eyes. She wondered whether he was a detective or whether wine tasting was his hobby.

Mouth feel and aftertaste are evoked by tannins. Tannins come from grape skins as well as stems, and if too strong are indicative of wines that are quite aged. Tannins also contribute to the bitterness. **Tannins are typical of red wines.** Tannins are also found in tea, chocolate, and skins of fruit. The more common mouthfeel sensations of wine include astringent, leathery, or velvety coating, puckery, drying, and tingling. Experts can also pick up texture such as grainy, chalky, dusty, furry, silky, puckery, chewy, steely, and soapy.

The final decision of a wine's quality, however, is always up to you – while you can be better trained to describe the flavor and aroma of different wines, it is your personal opinion that guides your own enjoyment of wine.

EXAMPLE

The officer pulled his partner aside and explained: "At the investigation, she said he drugged her with the wine he gave her at dinner. She said the wine had a strong blackberry, oaken flavor – that she could not have noticed it was tampered with. But the wine glasses we found on the table that night had a lemony colored liquid in them. Something is wrong – her story just doesn't check out. Let's tell the D.A."

White wines tend to be more floral and citrusy, whereas red wines tend to be more berry-like, spicy (black pepper, anise) and earthy or oaken. Wine can be sweet or sour tasting. Some of the most common aromas are fruity (blackberry, raspberry, strawberry, peach, apple, plum, apricot, banana), oak-woody, musty, and vinegar. Other aromas include grapey, buttery, minty, spicy (peppery, licorice, cloves) nutty, bell pepper, smoky, vanilla, moldy, earthy, grassy, hay-straw, green, alcoholic, medicinal, floral (violet, rose, geranium), citrusy, green olive, black olive, and orange. Chilled wine brings out its sweetness and acidity, and suppresses its aroma. Sparkling wines are carbonated and have citrusy (lime), vanilla, malty, caramel, nutmeg, apple, cherry, and strawberry aromas. The "body" of the wine is the heaviness or thickness or viscosity of the wine.

You do not have to consume wine to obtain its descriptions. You can visit a store that has a broad selection of wines and record what's on the labels. For example, the label on a Merlot might read: oaky, toasted vanilla, blackberry, and plum lingering aroma with a soft velvety finish. A Cabernet Sauvignon might be described as: blackberry, cinnamon, and oaky aroma with a dry taste and strong tannin, long finish. A white Riesling might have a citrus, peach, apricot, and floral description.

YOUR TURN

Finish the scene:

I was given the dream job for a detective – undercover as a wine taster. I arrived early to get the most out of this assignment, considering that many of the wines were beyond my affordability. I watched judges sip, slurp, swirl and spit. Yes, spit! When I stepped up to the first exhibit, which featured Chilean wines, I . . .

The Body of a Good Beer

Many people who drink beer claim to know their favorite brands. I tested this on my friends who claimed, "There's only one beer I drink. I don't like any others." So I set up ten beers in large, plastic, blue cups with aluminum foil covers. I gave out ten cards with the names of the beers on them. My friends had to match the beers to the names on the cards. The two extremes were a heavy stout beer and a non-alcoholic beer. They did quite well with these. But in between these two extremes, they found it almost impossible to match the names to the beers.

Beer is simply a combination of malted barley, hops, water, and yeast. The yeast ferments the sugar of the grain to form alcohol. This process produces beer and ale. **Lager and pilsner beers** are light-bodied, straw-colored, carbonated beers familiar to most Americans. There are pale, amber, and dark lagers. Ales are technically different than beers because they use different yeast. **Pale and dark ales** are fuller bodied with more alcohol content. **A porter or a stout** beer, which has greater alcohol content than most beers, is dark brown-colored with a roasted barley flavor and a bitter taste. The appearance of a beer (e.g., color, cloudiness) and carbonation are important to its flavor. For tasting, beer should be served at 50-60° Fahrenheit.

EXAMPLE

He tipped his pint of roasted dark stout to her glass of pale lager as the crowd in the tavern cheered and hugged each other – the bells of New Year's Eve rang and the adoration in his heart grew for the fine young lady who sat before him.

Beer and ale are comprised of many naturally-produced chemicals that contribute to a variety of flavors and aftertaste. These products are evaluated by taste experts for appearance (color, foam head, cloudiness, carbonation), aroma, flavor, and body (such as light- or full-bodied). The tastes of beer can include sour or acidic, sweet, salty, and bitter. The flavors in a beer are a result of the malt and grains used to produce it – giving it a malty, grainy, or nutty flavor. Other flavors include: aromatic, fragrant, fruity, apples, caramelized, roasted, burnt, smoky, phenolic, medicinal, fatty, oily, buttery, rancid, sulfury, corn, yeasty, musty, papery, moldy, and earthy. When grains are roasted they provide the beer with a caramel and roasted malt flavor, and a darker color. A dry beer lacks residual sugar while a fruity beer contains residual sugar. The presence of residual sugar affects its flavor. Light beers (lager and pilsner) have little body and few flavors, while dark beers could have any combination of these descriptions.

There is more to beer than the grains it is made from. Alcohol imparts an alcoholic flavor. **Hops provide the bitter taste** and spicy, pine, herbal, grassy aroma. Hops from different growers differ, with some being more bitter and others being more herbal in effects. The mouthfeel sensations of beer include creamy, carbonated, astringent, metallic, flat, alcoholic, soapy, and mouth coating. A good foam "head" on a freshly poured glass of beer should be noticed – if the glass has residual oils or is not clean, the head may be flat.

> **EXAMPLE**
>
> *He popped the cap off the green bottle of warm beer that he had grabbed from the back of the pickup. Its skunky odor wafted up to her nose, reminding her of the rainy night they had rolled over into a ditch when he had swerved to avoid hitting a moose in the middle of the road.*

The quality of a beer's raw materials, its production, as well as its storage will affect its flavor. **Undesirable flavors** can develop, and they include rancid, sulfury, fishy, buttery, yeasty, stale, soapy, and skunky. Beer in green bottles, exposed to sunlight, can develop a skunky odor from the interaction between ultraviolet rays and organic matter in the beer.

Beer can be served "on tap" or as unpasteurized beer in kegs into which are tapped spigots for serving the beer. Beer can also be served in bottles. Canned beer is usually not served in a restaurant. Beer on tap can be served in 8 oz glasses or "pints" (16 oz glasses) or in pitchers (for larger groups of people). In America, beer is served well-chilled. Pale lagers tend to be served colder while dark ales and stouts tend to be served warmer.

> EXAMPLE
>
> *She had never been in such a fancy inn before tonight. The beer menu alone was intimidating – German, Belgium, and American beers; some on tap and some in bottles; lagers, ales, and stouts. The only beer she knew was the six-pack her father had brought home on Friday nights. If this was the beer selection, how would she make it through the dinner menu?*

One way to research the descriptions of beer or ale is to have lunch at a micro-brewery or upscale tavern that has a large menu of international beers. They might be able to provide a menu with ratings and descriptions of the beers. Even if you do not order any beer, but enjoy the food with an iced tea, you can get ideas for your story from the descriptions of beer on the menu. Another way to obtain information about beer flavor is through the Internet. Search for "**beer flavor wheel.**" The flavor wheel is an organized, logical sorting of the tastes, odors, and mouthfeel sensations that can be found in beer.

YOUR TURN

Finish the scene:

The car pulled over to the side of the road and stopped. I pulled up behind it and called in the plate. I put on my brights and walked up alongside the Chevy. The driver rolled down his window, and when he spoke . . .

Off Flavors in Fish

Fish was an important food in Bible times. God's people moaned about the boring taste of manna, desiring the good taste of fish (Num. 11:5). Jesus and His disciples enjoyed eating fish (Mark 6:41; Luke 24:41-42; John 21:7-14). One of the gates to the City of David was called the Fish Gate (2 Chron. 33:14; Neh. 12:39). And Jesus used the image of fishing, or catching fish, to call for His disciples to become fishers of men.

Fish can develop flavors from the water in which they live. The same fish grown in different waters – such as Atlantic salmon and Pacific salmon – acquire differences in flavor. Some food fish such as catfish, salmon, and trout are grown in fish ponds – this is called aquaculture. Prior to harvesting the fish from a pond, the buyer will microwave samples in a paper bag and taste the fish. **Trained fish tasters look for "taints" or off flavors.** Pond-raised fish can take on musty or earthy odors from algae growing in the ponds. Products from algae, microorganisms that produce decay, fish waste, and man-made pollution can affect the taste of fish. We all know that dead fish can stink up a lake, or even the Nile as recorded in Exodus 7:21.

EXAMPLE

Dad came home from opening day of trout season bragging about his catch – rainbows, browns and brookies. On Saturday he grilled some. "Nothing like wild trout!" he said. But when mom tasted her filet, she gave him this strange look, pointing her fork at him. Mine tasted a little dirt-like or moldy, but I figured that was only natural seeing as how the fish came from a natural stream in the mountains.

Fresh fish brought in from the sea are kept on ice to deter decomposition, and are served as soon as possible (within a week). If a fish cannot be served fresh, it should be gutted and stored in a freezer. Off flavors can come from detergents, wrapping materials, the ice it is stored with, and the cutting board used when handling the fish. Unacceptable flavors (fishy, rancid, fatty, wet cardboard) come from prolonged storage. Other off flavors (oniony, sulfury, sewage, decaying vegetation, rotten, moldy, woody, piney) come from decomposition from not being stored properly.

You should smell and taste fish meat while it's warm. Also, taste different parts of the filet. **The fishy flavor is strongest in meat from just under the skin.** Acceptable flavors include: mild fish flavor, corn, nutty, buttery, and chicken meat-like. Other flavors include celery, mushroom, grassy, and fish oil.

YOUR TURN

Finish the scene:

The blackout hit the restaurants the hardest in this seaside resort. Tons of scallops, crabs, flounder, red snapper and all kinds of seafood were bucketed into dumpsters. As the health inspector it was my job to . . .

There will be a Feast

As Christian writers and speakers, we are called to flavor our words with spiritual truth. We are called to serve the Lord with passion and boldness. We are not to be part of our society by simply preventing its deterioration (Rev. 3:15-16). We are to redeem the world for Christ: to be salt – not just for preserving but for bringing out the aroma of life, which is Christ. As the Bible draws on sensory imagery to enlighten us with spiritual mystery and awe, thus we too can draw on the Bible's rich use of sensory imagery to ignite a spark in the hearts of our audiences wherein the Spirit can perform miracles.

We have only just begun to appreciate what God has given us in our senses; there is so much more to learn. It would be a shame to relegate our senses to the basement of our daily existence. Rather, let us bring our senses to face the world head on, just as the nose on our face stands sentinel to a created world that is alive and wonderful to behold.

In our daily lives we show little conscious awareness of how much we depend on our senses. As babies, we come into the world of a sensory wonderland. For example, a mother's diet affects her amniotic fluid such that the unborn baby develops taste preferences. Once the baby is born, the mother's milk continues to expose the baby to her diet as the milk carries the flavor of the foods she eats. The child will continue to grow with exposure to touch, taste, hearing, smell, and sight. God also calls us to use our senses to grow and mature and become more like Christ.

The Bible refers directly to the senses of taste, smell, touch, vision, and hearing. For example, faith comes by hearing (Rom. 10:17). The name Ishmael means "God hears" (Gen. 3:9). Jesus touched the sick to heal them (Matt. 14:35-36; Mark 8:22-25). For sight, the Word is a light unto our path and Jesus is the light of the world (Matt. 5:14; 1 John 1:5-7). Our God is a God who sees (Gen. 6:11). We are encouraged to taste and see that the Lord is good (Ps. 34:8). The application of our senses has always carried with it a call to be discerning – to discern between the things of this world and the things of God.

However, in this fallen world, our senses are distorted, even at times dysfunctional. The sense of smell can be subject to anosmia, cacosmia, dysosmia, heterosmia, hyposmia, parosmia, phantosmia and even synesthesia. In a spiritual sense, through sin we lose our ability to hear properly and exercise discernment, and as a result we lose God's blessings (Deut. 4:48; Isa. 6:8-10; Amos 8:11-12). In the Garden of Eden, the serpent enticed Eve with a delicious, beautiful fruit – using her senses to draw her closer.

Our sensory experiences in this life provide a foretaste of what is to come. The Old Testament is full of feasts such as Passover, and the feasts of unleavened bread and first fruits. Communion is a feast of the New Testament and it draws on many of the human senses: we taste the bread, we enjoy the aroma of wine, we hear the Word preached, we see and touch one another. Feasts prepare God's people for the coming of the Master of the Banquet (Luke 14:12-24), who will one day provide a great wedding feast for His church. Our words, well-flavored, can be like save-the-date notices that engaged couples send out to friends and family – notices to not forget that a banquet is being prepared and that all believers are invited to attend (Rev. 22:17).

5
Sound and Body Balance

John Steinbeck –
The Grapes of Wrath

It was still dark when he awakened. A small clashing noise brought him up from sleep. Tom listened and heard again the squeak of iron on iron. He moved stiffly and shivered in the morning air. The camp still slept. Tom stood up and looked over the side of the truck. The eastern mountains were blueblack, and as he watched, the light stood up faintly behind them, colored at the mountain rims with a washed red, then growing colder, grayer, darker, as it went up overhead until at a place near the western horizon it merged with pure night. Down in the valley the earth was the lavender-green of dawn.
(New York, 1984: Penguin), 318-319

Understanding Audition

> **EXAMPLE**
>
> The rental car turned up the highway toward the Rockies. "Sure, son, go ahead and put on your music. My ears haven't popped since we got off the plane. Enjoy it while you can. Once we get to the ranch I'll be back to normal and all you'll be hearing is the wind in the aspens."

In order to hear, you receive sound waves, organize sound bits, and interpret the information. The outer ear collects sound that moves through air in waves, similar to waves on a lake. The eardrum in the **middle ear** is a membrane that responds to sound waves, transferring the vibrations to the hammer, anvil, and stirrup bones, which amplify the sound and in turn transfer it to the cochlea. The cochlea in the **inner ear** is filled with fluid that picks up the intensity and frequency of sound vibrations from the ear drum. Hair cells in the cochlea sense the vibrations and forward it to the auditory nerve, which carries it to the brain. It's an amazing system!

The fact that you have two ears helps you tell which direction sound is coming from – sound waves do not reach both ears at the same time unless you are facing the source of the sound head on or the sound is coming from directly behind you. Try bending your ears toward the front of your face, with cupped hands over your ears in the direction of a sound. Notice how this enhances the sound.

The three main components of sound that your ear distinguishes

are **frequency, loudness, and pitch.** Since sound moves through the air in compression waves, frequency is the number of waves per second. Loudness is the amplitude of the waves. Pitch is the tonal quality.

EXAMPLE

I heard a piercing screech as she reached for her right ear. I hadn't noticed she had a hearing aid. She turned away, embarrassed. I turned toward her, "It's okay." Actually, it was more than okay. Maybe she hadn't heard that stupid comment I'd made in the diner. Now I could start all over without worrying that she had heard me.

Hearing problems can be temporary or permanent. Tinnitus causes a ringing or buzzing sound in your ears after being exposed to a loud noise. Loud noises cause damage to the ear's mechanisms and can cause hearing loss. The middle ear is prone to ear infections such as otitis media. When fluid or pus builds up behind the eardrum it can lead to infections. Wax in the outer ear can lead to hearing loss, too. Hearing is so important for language and effective communication that hearing problems can lead to depression and feelings of isolation.

As you age, your ear drum thickens, hair cells die off, and high frequency sounds become harder to pick up so that when someone is talking quickly, or there are echoes, or you are in a crowded room, you may have trouble understanding what you are hearing. **Hearing aids help counteract chronic or permanent hearing loss.** You can have one hearing aid or two for your ears. Hearing aids vary in how they fit into the ear; some are more noticeable in appearance than others.

YOUR TURN

Finish the scene:

One of the students was tone deaf. His mom confessed that about him. There was no other way to pick him out from the crowded room and loud music. I couldn't just yell out, "Tom!" So I moved about the dance floor listening for . . .

Faith Comes by Hearing

God calls us to hear and to speak to Him; God Himself speaks (2 Kings 18:12) and hears (2 Kings 19:16). Adam and Eve heard God walking in Eden and God heard them (Gen. 3:8, 10). God's voice thunders, breaks cedar trees, and is powerful (Ps. 29:3-5).

Worship is a time of hearing. We hear the voices of God's people singing praise, shouting for joy, and even weeping. Sometimes we hear the quiet – the silence of God. We hear the Word preached and the declarations of faith from those who are saved. It is a mystery to us that the Spirit of God accomplishes God's plan for salvation through the Word in both written and spoken forms.

If we are born of God by faith, we will hear God speak and we will recognize His voice (John 5:25; John 8:47; John 10:3-5; 1 John 4:6; Rev. 3:20; Rev. 22:17). God spoke to His leaders (Ex. 19:19; Isa. 5:9) and helped them in turn speak the truth (Ex. 4:12). And the truth of God, the witness of His love for His people, spread by word of mouth, or from ear to ear (Ps. 44:1).

God will turn a deaf ear at times. God does not promise to hear the voice of sinners who choose to turn away from Him (John 9:31). If we are not born of God through faith but rather choose rebellion, or to live in sin, we will be deaf to Him or dull in hearing the truth (Ps. 38:13; Isa. 43:8; Matt. 13:15; Acts 28:27).

But there is hope. **Jesus brought healing to those who were deaf or dull in hearing** (Mark 7:33-37; Luke 7:22). This also refers to spiritual hearing, which we obtain by faith in Jesus (Matt. 11:15; Matt. 13:9). Therefore, we must not refuse to hear God when He speaks to us (Heb. 12:25).

Write an Outline to Practice Speaking about *Speaking and Listening to God* using the following Bible verses:

- Genesis 3:10
- 2 Kings 18:12
- 2 Kings 19:16
- Psalm 29:3-5
- Psalm 38:13
- Psalm 44:1
- Matthew 13:9
- John 9:31
- John 10:3-5
- Acts 28:27
- Hebrews 12:25
- 1 John 4:6

The Ear and Body Balance

Your inner ear consists of canals or chambers filled with fluid, oriented at right angles to each other in three planes of rotation. This alignment allows you to determine **pitch** (movement of the head in a "yes" manner), **roll** (tumbling left or right), and **yaw** (movement of the head in a "no" manner). As your head moves, the fluid shifts, causing tiny hairs to detect this and alert your brain. When this action backfires, though, you experience motion sickness. With age, the hairs die off and you become more unsteady, showing disequilibrium and even vertigo and nausea.

When your ears pop there is a change in air pressure. **Eustachian tubes** connect the back of your nose to your middle ear, and open or pop to adjust pressure inside your middle ear behind the eardrum. Swallowing helps to open the tubes to let air in. When air pressure on both sides of the eardrum is unequal, you feel as if your ears are blocked – sounds are muffled. If the blockage continues, fluid is drawn into the ear tubes causing more problems ("fluid in the ear"). Swallowing, yawning, or chewing gum activates muscles that help open the tubes. Colds, sinus infections, and nasal allergies can promote blockage by deterring the opening of the tubes and proper drainage.

> **EXAMPLE**
>
> *Seven men and women lined up against the wall. Their faces were dirty, bloody, and exhausted. Their faces were also proud and defiant. The interrogator examined each with his eyes. He walked down the line sniffing. He listened to their breathing. Then he brought them one by one to the center of the courtyard, had them hold a broom above their heads, and spin in a circle until he fired a shot from his pistol.*
>
> *"That one, he's the pilot. Bring him to my office."*
>
> *Six returned to their cells. One was escorted to the office of the interrogator.*

Did you ever play the game of spinning around in a circle, suddenly stopping, and then trying to stand still? You stumbled and fell down. The fluid in your inner ear kept spinning even though you stopped. Your brain tried to compensate, but you lost your balance.

YOUR TURN

Finish the scene:

The woman we were searching for had just flown cross country and was one of the people in line to board a jet for Canada. There was one woman with a wrinkled blouse, and messy hair who . . .

Where to Find Sounds of Life

Libraries afford writers an opportunity to study sound. Although libraries are quiet, everyday life movements take place there – chairs shift, people walk and sit, doors open, and books close. The library contains a wide range of materials – wood, metal, leather, paper, rubber, cloth – that make different sounds that go unnoticed when they are buried beneath the noisy chatter of life's activities. In the quietness of the library, sounds of life reappear.

You can hear the sound that rubber soles make on wood flooring, pressed down by over-weight or slender bodies. Listen as leather soled shoes pass by. Do they slap the wood or shuffle or slide? Do they sound different on marble versus tile flooring? Listen as the librarian opens a metal drawer, glides across the floor on the rollers of an old wooden office chair to speak in a low voice over the telephone. Two students whisper as one taps 3x5 cards together and snaps a rubber band around them. A wheelchair squishes down the hallway toward the bathroom. A computer keyboard pops and taps to the fingers of a student who searches online for an author's work.

Did you know that hardback books sound different from paperback books? Hardback books thud closed, whereas paperback books close with a flipping sound. Newspaper pages rustle, whereas magazine pages crinkle. Books being stacked sound different from books being shelved.

> EXAMPLE
>
> *My story was at a turning point......*
>
> *I was startled out of a deep sleep by a sound that was an echo from my past. Jerking up to a sitting position, I pulled the covers closer. Staring into the darkness, barely breathing, I waited for the sound to reappear. Had it really happened or was it part of a forgotten dream?*
>
> *Again. In the hallway on the other side of my bedroom door. It was real. My mind spun through its circular files of sound cards to recall the origin, the owner, the cause. I knew I'd heard it before – some distant, buried memory that brought chills to the back of my neck.*
>
> *Then writer's block stopped me cold. A TV droned downstairs in the living room. A housefly buzzed and beat against the window screen, trying to escape. A German Shepherd howled at a passing ambulance. The turning point of my story was in need of a sound and I was stranded. Where could I turn to find the authentic sound I needed?*

I went to my city's public library to make a list of sounds. Here is what I recorded within an hour's time:

- A metallic jingle of keys dangling on an ID badge's chain, hanging around the neck of a security guard.
- A metal-to-metal hollow tinkling clink of keys hanging off the belt of a maintenance man.
- A clap of dry sneakers on marble steps compared to the squishy slap of wet sneakers on tiled floor.
- The heal-to-toe beat of a healthy stride compared to the heavy, flat-footed clop of a middle-aged, out-of-shape man.
- The difference between heal-to-toe walking on a flat floor and toe-to-heal walking on steps.

- A flip-flop or flop-flip of sandals depending on whether the right or left leg is favored.
- A squeaky, gritty scrape of wooden chair on a tiled floor compared to the gritty groan of wooden chair on a wood floor.
- A high pitched whistle of a stool's metal leg on tiled floor, like the sound of a distant train whistle.
- The hollow thump of hardback book onto the plastic book-return cart.
- The crispy crackle of a thin plastic bag.
- The click-click of a pen being opened and closed.

EXERCISE

Set your alarm clock for 3 AM. When you awake, take a note pad and sit in your living room and listen. Record the sounds of the night. Your hearing will adjust the way your eyes do after you've been in the dark for some time. See if you pick up different sounds than during the day. Make a list of those sounds:

1.

2.

3.

4.

5.

6.

7.

8.

Help in Describing Sounds

Do you need a sound for your story? Perhaps you need a mysterious sound such as buzzing, creaking, fizzing, inharmonic, murmuring, scratching, or whirring. Or maybe you are searching for a novel description of a noise. If you get stuck on a sound, here is a list of descriptions that could be used for sounds in all sorts of situations:

A   Abrading, abrasive, acoustic, aflutter, airy, alternating, amplified, articulate, audible.

B   Babbling, banging, baritone, barking, barraging, bashing, battering, beating, belching, bell-like, belting, biting, blaring, blasting, blattering, blowing, blubbering, boiling, bombing, booming, bopping, bounding, braying, breaking, breathing, brushing, bubbling, buckling, buffing, bumping, bursting, busting, bustling, buzzing.

C   Cackling, catty, chanting, chattering, chatty, chewing, chilling, chiming, chirpy, chittering, choir-like, choking, chopping, chortling, chuckling, clamoring, clanging, clanking, clapping, clattering, clearing, cleaving, clicking, climbing, clinking, clipping, closing, clubbing, clucking, clumping, clunking, combusting, cooing, coughing, cracking, crackling, cranking, crashing, creaking, crinkling, crumbling, crunching, crying, cutting.

D   Denting, digging, dipping, disploding, dissonant, dribbling, drilling, dripping, dropping, drumming.

E Eating, echoing, erasing, erupting, exhaling, exploding.

F Fading, falling, fanning, fiddling, fissuring, fizzing, flailing, flapping, fleeting, flipping, flip-flopping, flopping, flowing, flumping, flushing, fluting, fluttering, frizzing, fuming.

G Gagging, gangling, gimping, gliding, gnashing, gnawing, grating, grinding, gritty, groaning, growling, gruff, grumbling, grunting, gurgling, gushing, guttural.

H Hacking, hammering, hobbling, hollow, honking, hooting, howling, humming.

I Imploding, inflating, inhaling, inharmonic, interlude, interrupting, intoning, irreproducible.

J Jabbing, jamming, jarring, jigging, jingling, jittering, jolting, jumping.

K Kicking, knocking.

L Lapping, laryngeal, lashing, laughing, leaking, leaping, licking, lilting, limping, locking, loud, lumbering.

M Marching, melodious, merry, metallic, metronomic, miming, moaning, modulating, monotone, mourning, moving, mowing, muffled, munching, murmuring, musical, mute, muttering, muzzled.

N Nearby, noisy, nonstop, noticeable.

O Orchestral.

P Pacifiable, paddling, palpitating, panting, patting, pausing, pawing, pealing, pecking, peeping, pelting, penetrating, perceptible, percussive, periodic, phonic, piercing, piping, plodding, polyrhythmic, popping, pounding, pulsating.

R Rapping, raspy, rattling, rending, repercussive, repetitious, resonant, rhythmic, ringing, ripping, rippling, roaring, rocking, rotating, rubbing, ruffling, rumbling, running, rushing, rustling.

S Sanding, sawing, scraping, scratching, screaming screeching, scribbling, scrubbing, scuffling, scurrying, shaking, shattering, shooting, shredding, shrill, shrieking, shuffling, shushing, sighing, silent, singing, skating, skidding, slamming, slapping, slashing, sliding, sipping, slipping, slithering, sloshing, slugging, slurring, slurping, slushing, smacking, smashing, snapping, snarling, sneaking, sneezing, sniffing, sniffling, snipping, snoring, snorting, snuffing, sobbing, songful, sonic, sonorous, soundless, spanking, spatting, spattering, spilling, spitting, splashing, splattering, splintering, splitting, spluttering, spooky, springing, sprinkling, sprinting, sputtering, squeaking, squishing, stamping, stapling, static, stepping, stereophonic, sticking, strangling, striking, strumming, stuttering, subvocal, sucking, surprising, sustained, swallowing, swarming, swatting, sweeping, swinging, swooshing, symphonious.

T Talking, tamping, tapping, tearing, thrashing, threshing, thrilling, throaty, thrusting, thundering, ticking, tinkling, tinny, tolling, tooting, tornadic, tramping, trampling, transient, treading, trembling, tromping, tumbling, tuneful, twittering, typewriting.

U Ultrasonic, unpronounced, unutterable, upchucking, uproarious, uptempo, uttering.

V Variable, vaulting, venting, ventilating, verbose, vibrant, vibrating, violent, vociferating, voicing, volcanic.

W Waddling, wading, wafting, wagging, waggling, wailing, walking, walloping, wambling, wangling, warring, warbling, warning, washing, watering, weaving, wedging, weeping, wetting, whacking, whamming, wheezing, whiffling, whimpering, whinnying, whipping, whirring, whispering, whistling, whittling, whizzing, whomping, whooping, whooshing, whopping, winding, wiping, woodworking, wrapping, wrestling, wriggling, wringing, wrinkling, writing.

Y Yakking, yapping, yawning, yawp, yelling, yelping, yipping.

Z Zapping, zippering, zooming.

EXERCISE

From the above list of sounds, select three that describe each of the following events:

A) A children's birthday party
   1.
   2.
   3.

B) A carpenter's workshop
   1.
   2.
   3.

C) An autobody garage
   1.
   2.
   3.

D) A police shoot out
   1.
   2.
   3.

E) A large family holiday dinner
   1.
   2.
   3.

6
Touch, Pain And Expressions

J.R.R. Tolkien –
The Hobbit

The yells and yammering, croaking, jibbering and jabbering; howls, growls and curses; shrieking and skriking, that followed were beyond description. Several hundred wild cats and wolves being roasted slowly alive together would not have compared with it. The sparks were burning holes in the goblins, and the smoke that now fell from the roof made the air too thick for even their eyes to see through. Soon they were falling over one another and rolling in heaps on the floor, biting and kicking and fighting as if they had all gone mad.
(New York: Ballantine Books, 1977), 72

Touch is Very Important

The skin is the body's largest sensory organ – it has receptors for touch (tactile sense), pressure, pain, and temperature. Sensory information is provided by nerve endings in the skin's surface and deeper tissue, hair follicles, sweat glands, and blood vessels. A hair follicle is situated within skin such that by brushing hair you can feel. Pressure is a result of the bending and stretching of the skin, its pores and nerve endings. The greatest number of receptors are the nerves that give you the sense of pain. Tissue damage to the skin results in pain. The sense of touch also exists internally – you can feel pain from sensations in your throat, lungs, stomach, and intestines for example.

Your fingertips, lips, and tongue have the greatest number of nerve endings. The tongue is sensitive to touch – it allows you to detect the crispiness of foods (food texture), the hot spiciness of hot peppers, and changes in temperature.

Certain receptors are particularly sensitive to a **gentle touch**. These are found on the palms of your hands and soles of your feet, as well as on your lips, eyelids, genitalia, and nipples. Women tend to have more receptors to pain than men.

Tactile defensiveness is an over-reaction to touch. This could be triggered from being touched or from touching someone or something. It can be so extreme as to cause fear. **Anesthesia** is the inability to feel the sense of touch. **Paresthesia** is a feeling of being touched when nothing is happening to cause the sensation.

> **EXAMPLE**
>
> *We rescued the infant from an orphanage. No one knew her mother or where she came from. She spoke very little and would not make eye contact. She seemed depressed and isolated. When I reached out to stroke her arm she flinched as if I pricked her with a pin. I could only imagine what it was like growing up without the nurturing touch of a mother.*

The cold receptors are most abundant on the tips of your nose, lips, and forehead. There are separate receptors for cold and hot because it is critical for the skin to adjust to changes in temperature. Your skin, in communication with your brain, tries to keep your body temperature between 97° F to 99° F (36.5° to 37° C), avoiding hyperthermia and hypothermia. Sweat glands release body vapor and with it, body heat, to cool the body. If it's too cold, your body will shiver to warm up.

The sensations of cold and hot are described in the Bible. First, God created summer and winter, hot and cold seasons (Gen. 8:22). Yet in a spiritual sense, God hates lukewarm people – He wants us to stand our ground and show whether we are hot or cold to His love (Rev. 3:15). If we are spiritually cold to God, and unrepentant of sin and rebellion, God's breath can be icy upon us (Job 37:9-10), or His anger can burn (Judges 3:8) or His judgment will consume like a fire (Rev. 16:8-9) just as sin consumes like a hot oven (Hosea 7:3-7).

YOUR TURN

Finish the scene:

I closed my eyes and listened to the chirping birds, with the breeze rustling through the leaves hanging loosely in the trees. I hadn't felt this free since I was a child – these feelings of . . .

Pain is Quite Complex

> **EXAMPLE**
>
> *As the grieving mother explained to me what had happened two years ago, how her son had been killed by a thief who stabbed him in the chest, I watched her clutch her hands to her own chest. Her breathing became difficult. So I ordered an X ray. She smiled. I didn't know what else to do or say.*

Pain is an experience that arises from complex interactions involving your memory, emotions, and subconscious. If pain is linked to a horrible memory or emotion, it can be heightened. Somatoform disorder is where negative emotions bring about actual symptoms of pain. Hyperalgesia is a disorder marked by an increased sensitivity to pain.

Although we all deal with pain, the world of science and medicine know all too little about pain. Pain is complicated. It has many causes and includes subjective aspects that make it difficult to measure the level of pain from person to person.

Pain can be described as a sensory system in itself. It involves pressure, temperature, and chemical changes. It can result from changes internal to your body or from problems occurring on the surface of your body. There are three different receptors or nerves for pain, ranging from an acute, sharp pain to a dull lingering pain. Pain can be a warning sensation; or it can be a chronic or lasting ache. Pain may be movement-related such that it only flares up with specific body movements.

Physical pain is referred to in three aspects:

- There is first or **fast pain**: This pain lasts as long as the nerves are stimulated. For example, when you bend a finger backwards you feel the pain. As soon as you stop bending it backwards, the pain stops.
- There is second or **slow pain**: This pain persists and spreads out from the site of origination such as when you break a leg.
- Finally, there is **phantom pain**: A person who lost a limb, as by amputation, can experience a Phantom Limb Sensation. This is where phantom sensations from nerve endings and receptors continue to tell the brain that the limb is attached. Phantom sensations can also occur with a lost tooth or missing eye.

Chronic pain is believed to develop when the brain and spinal system of nerves establish a memory of a painful experience. As you age, you tend to acquire chronic pain such as from headaches, back pain, and knee or joint problems. Chronic pain is a serious problem. Chronic pain increases overall stress and interferes with life's activities (e.g., sleep, relaxation, concentration at work, and socialization).

A common cause of acute or chronic pain is a knee disorder (a problem with muscles, ligaments, tendons, or cartilage). This includes arthritis and sports accidents, which can appear days, months, or years later. Pain can occur after sitting for a time or when exercising the knee. Climbing stairs is particularly hard on the knees. Runners, soccer players, skaters, cyclists, and dancers often exhibit knee problems as they age. Symptoms include a clicking or popping of the joint, morning stiffness, a locking of the knee, a buckling out or failure of the knee to support weight, or a swollen joint.

EXAMPLE

A group of middle-aged men came down the marble steps from the grand hall, laughing, and talking. The one I was looking for was the retired soccer player. The others were a banker, lawyer, and accountant. They all looked quite fit. But one grimaced as he came down step by step. He had to be the one I needed to see. The years of soccer would have taken a toll on his knees. And there was more pain I was about to inflict – pain he didn't know was coming.

Another well-known source of pain is the migraine headache. The actual cause is believed to be associated with restricted blood flow around the brain. It might flare up in children, teenagers, or people in their twenties and thirties. The frequency of occurrence can be weekly or once a year, and is more common in women than in men. A migraine can be brought on by a variety of events such as stress, changes in the weather, and certain foods. A migraine headache can develop on one side or both sides of your head. A classic migraine can last for one or two days with the following symptoms: flashing lights appear; vision is affected; legs become weak; speech is difficult; an intense throbbing or pounding appears in the forehead, ears, jaw, temple, or around the eyes. A common migraine can last for three to four days and have the following symptoms: nausea; upset stomach; mood change; and fatigue along with the headache.

EXAMPLE

I had two days left to complete my manuscript. It was not enough. The mold in this rustic hide-away cabin had given me a headache – a bad one. It was like the ones I used to get as a teenager after my dad moved my bedroom to the basement. It was a headache that made me sick to my stomach – that blurred my vision – radiating from one side of my head to the other. I could not focus. I could not work.

Part of any response to pain is an avoidance of situations that might bring on pain: The "Fight or Flight" reaction. This is where you decide to stay and fight, or to run away. In the instant of decision-making, your body changes: Heart rate increases to prepare for action; blood moves throughout your body more quickly, carrying oxygen; sweating increases to start cooling down your body; digestion slows to conserve energy; blood pressure increases; airways dilate to allow more efficient breathing; adrenaline is released to increase metabolism, which increases body temperature and the release of stored energy; and alertness is heightened.

Treatments for relieving pain are varied: acupuncture, biofeedback, music therapy, relaxation techniques, drugs, and opioids. Some of the commonly used drugs include morphine, the morphine derivative Kadian, Fentanyl as a skin patch, Vicodin, and OxyContin. People become addicted to pain relief medication.

When writing about pain, there are various ways to describe it. Some descriptions are more objective and some are more emotional. Here is a list of words to help you when you are looking for the right way to describe pain:

A Aching, agonizing, awful

B Beating, biting, blinding, burning

C Cutting, cramping, crushing

D Deafening, distracting, distressing, drilling

E Excruciating, exhausting

F Flashing, flinching, freezing

G Grinding, grueling

H Hurting

I Intense, intolerable, itching

L Lancinating

M Miserable

N Nagging, nauseating, numbing

P Piercing, pinching, pounding, pressing, pricking, pulsating

Q Quivering

R Radiating

S Scalding, searing, severe, sickening, sharp, shooting, smarting, sore, splitting, spreading, squeezing, stabbing, stinging, strong, suffocating

T Tickling, tingling, throbbing, torturing

U Unbearable, uncomfortable, unpleasant

W Wrenching

Another aspect of pain is the condition of your body when it receives injury. Your bones are constantly rebuilding, with a strength that reaches its peak in your twenties. While muscle building goes on into older age, bone building slows down. Activities affect how your muscles and bones develop – for example there are differences between athletes who swim and those who run. And all of this will affect the experience of pain.

The Bible speaks of the introduction of pain into the world through sin – our work will be painful and childbearing will be painful (Gen. 3:16-17). Judgment and sin brings forth pain and torment (Matt. 8:12; Matt. 25:30; Rev. 16:10-11; Rev. 20:10). Yet God has used pain to discipline or strengthen His people's faith (Job 33:19; Isa. 13:8; Isa. 26:17-18). Most importantly, we live with the hope that a day will come when there will be no more pain (Rev. 21:4).

EXERCISE

Consider the following events and match three descriptive words of pain for each event (but do not actually do the event yourself):

A) Slammed a door on your finger
   1.
   2.
   3.

B) Fell off a stage
   1.
   2.
   3.

C) Bit into a hot slice of pizza
   1.
   2.
   3.

D) Woke up with both arms and hands asleep
   1.
   2.
   3.

Healing Powers

It is well known that the sense of touch is critical to the healthy growth of an infant. We need to be held by our mothers and fathers. We need to touch one another and be touched – a hug, a holding of hands, a pat on the back, a hand shake. Normal emotional and physical growth as humans requires a lot of touching.

When Jesus walked the earth, people crowded around Him hoping to touch Him, even His clothing, to be healed (Matt. 9:20-21; Matt. 14:36; Mark 3:10; Mark 5:28; Luke 8:44). **Touch has always been important for healing.** Doctors today touch their patients. A good doctor will use her senses to make a thorough physical examination of her patient, especially when diagnosing a medical problem. Doctors cannot rely solely on computer-based charts and decision trees. They need to touch as well as see and smell and hear their patients.

Adam and Eve were forbidden to touch the fruit of one tree in the Garden of Eden (Gen. 3:3). God continued to warn us that there are things we should not touch – unclean things (Lev. 7:21; Lev. 11:8; Isa. 52:11; 2 Cor. 6:17). God warns us that there are holy things, too, that we should not touch (Num. 4:15; Ps. 105:15).

The Bible speaks of God's hand and touch, which can be mighty and convicting. The "finger of God" demonstrated His power to Pharaoh (Ex. 8:19), wrote the Ten Commandments on stone (Ex. 31:18), and drove out demons (Luke 11:20). Jesus wrote a message on the ground, using His finger, that convicted those who had ears to hear, but fell deaf on those who could not hear or see the truth (John 8:6-8).

> Write an Outline to Practice Speaking about *The Hand of God* using the following Bible verses:
>
> - Genesis 22:9-10
> - Exodus 8:19
> - Numbers 4:15
> - Matthew 9:21
> - Mark 5:28
> - Luke 11:20
> - Luke 22:69
> - John 3:35
> - John 8:6-8
> - John 10:28
> - John 20:25
> - 2 Corinthians 6:17

Perhaps the gentlest of touch is made with a kiss. Lips are very sensitive to touch. And when you kiss, you not only touch but you smell, hear, see, and sometimes taste the one you are kissing. Thus, kissing involves multiple senses in a very intimate way. However, throughout history, and in different cultures even today, kissing is not always something that is allowed to be done in public and or even at all. Nonetheless, God encouraged us to greet one another (our brothers or sisters in the Lord) with a holy kiss (Rom. 16:16; 2 Cor. 13:12). We are called to kiss the Son and praise the Lord (Ps. 2:12). By contrast, Judas betrayed Jesus with a kiss (Matt. 26:48; Luke 22:47-48).

Body Tremors

The Bible refers to the shaking and trembling of the body. Tremors of the arms and hands come from old age (Eccl. 12:3). A person can tremble in excitement (Mark 16:8) or in fear (Acts 16:29), especially in fear of God (2 Cor. 7:15). Moses trembled in fear of God (Heb. 12:21). Even the demons tremble in fear of God (James 2:19).

A tremor can be described as an involuntary, rhythmic oscillation of a body part or a muscle contraction. You likely have a barely noticeable or non-visible tremor that can become exaggerated under episodes of extreme cold or pain, stage freight, fatigue, stress, nervousness, or fever. Tremor can also be drug-induced, as with caffeine or heavy metal (e.g., lead or mercury) poisoning. Diseases can bring about tremor such as from hypoglycemia, central nervous system disorders, thyroid disorders, stroke, and multiple sclerosis. Psychological or psychiatric-associated tremors that affect any part of the body at rest or when moving can occur once or they can be chronic and are usually due to trauma, stress, and anxiety.

A **resting tremor** in which you have a tremor while at rest is Parkinson's Disease (PD), a neurologic disorder that lessens with movement but increases while resting. A **postural tremor** is when the body is held in a position against gravity such as when you extend out your arms from your body. This tremor is quite natural and often so slight you might not even notice it. However, it can become noticeable under medical symptoms, alcohol withdrawal, hypoglycemia, and so forth. A **kinetic tremor** is noticed when your body is moving, such as when writing, eating, and drinking. An **orthostatic tremor** appears after standing for a long time; when the legs cramp up and shake. The lower body can also shake and you can feel unsteady. Finally, an **isometric tremor** is noticed when you contract your muscles such as by squeezing something with your hand.

Some people have **Restless Legs Syndrome**. At night they feel pins and needles in their legs. The discomfort is relieved by movement. They might show signs of twitching while sleeping.

> ### EXAMPLE
>
> *Grandma sat in her chair as usual, across from me, with white thinning hair and a pale, wrinkled face. Her head shook in a no-no manner as if she were pondering something – but I think she was unaware of the shaking. Grandpa seemed unconcerned. I couldn't help but notice. I think my head started to shake like hers. I tried thinking of school or basketball and looked down at my feet to take my mind off of it.*

Essential Tremor (ET) is a benign, hereditary tremor that increases with age. There is typically a family history for someone who has ET. It causes involuntary, rhythmical trembling. Many people have ET and never go to a doctor to have it diagnosed. Many people do not know they have ET because the tremor is so slight. It has been estimated to affect about 10 million Americans. A little alcohol lessens it for a time but holding something up against gravity heightens it. It can be a tremor of the hands, head (yes-yes or no-no movement), legs, or voice.

YOUR TURN

Finish the scene:

Erin followed the Senator all day, beginning at 5 AM. Finally, she caught him between a courthouse and his limo. "Senator – can I have a minute of your time?" She held up the microphone with two hands – cold, stressed out, tired, and nervous . . .

Facial Expressions

The face is a very complicated matrix of nerves and muscles that provide movement of the jaw, mouth, lips, and eyebrows, allowing you to open and close your eyes and wrinkle your forehead. Facial muscles produce around 43 movements, which in turn create over 10,000 unique expressions. These movements help you protect your face, express emotion, breathe, eat, talk, see, smell, and yawn. Facial expressions include: blank, frown, glare, laughter, pout, shock, smile, smirk, sneer, snarl, excitement, joy, puzzlement, grief, horror, peace, pain, comic, and distorted.

> **EXAMPLE**
>
> *I made a list of emotions and taped it to the wall beside the mirror. Every day for a month I practiced an emotion. Even though I was auditioning for a bit part in the play, I wanted to make an impression. Monday I practiced anger. On Tuesday, surprise. Wednesday, a frown. Thursday, happiness. On Friday, sadness. Saturday, fear and Sunday I practiced relief.*

Your face is determined at birth – your bone structure and arrangement of tissue about the bones – the eyes and brows, nose, mouth and lips, chin, cheeks, forehead, and ears. But changes do occur over time (as with wrinkles), with health problems (allergies, skin conditions), and medical problems (stroke, nerve damage, accidents, and scars). Nerve damage or brain damage can cause partial paralysis of one side of the face or it can reduce facial expressions in general.

The face is critical for communication and the development of relationships. Facial expressions affect your social comfort as well as your feelings of security and success. Thus, facial muscles have been mapped to help experts better understand expression.

> **EXAMPLE**
>
> *Jackson didn't look in the perp's face when his partner was questioning him. Jackson was not good at reading faces. Faces threw him off track. Rather, he sensed whether a person was lying by watching body movements and listening. Jackson had the gift of unusual accuracy in nailing a perp – as good as any lie detector.*

Facial expressions provide critical non-verbal communication and are linked to emotions. Some people are uncomfortable seeing a person's face because they over-react to facial expressions. Some people can hide an emotional expression (such as with a "poker face") or make up an emotional expression to some degree. This is what actors do for a living. Facial expressions can be very slight such that you respond to them without realizing it, or they can be quite radical such as when you laugh, cry, or express horror. Facial expressions can be involuntary and subconscious, or voluntary and consciously produced.

Your day-to-day facial expressions as brought on by your emotions are basically independent of your culture or upbringing – they are universal, but with variations of expression. Ekman and Friesen at the University of California in San Francisco created a **Facial Action Coding System** or FACS, believing that facial expressions are universal and biologically determined. What does this mean for you as a writer? When your character feels guilt one moment and shame another, you should describe markedly different expressions. However, a character that shows frustration that leads to anger may not show a distinguishing difference in expression because these emotions are too closely linked.

Basic emotions can be divided into groups of similar emotions. One possible list gives six basic emotions: happiness, surprise, fear, sadness, anger, and disgust. Another list gives the following categories: amusement;

anger; contempt; contentment; disgust; embarrassment; excitement; fear; guilt; pride in achievement; relief; sadness/distress; satisfaction; sensory pleasure; and shame.

Learning how to recognize and reproduce facial expressions is important for artists and actors. It is also important for security and police personnel. **The muscles in the face respond quicker to emotion than you can control them**, and minute details can be recognized by trained people. You can see in microseconds the change in facial muscles before the person has a chance to control her expression – thus, much is done involuntarily or without thinking.

The accurate interpretation of facial expression is a very useful skill to develop. It is true that a liar's behavior can often "turn him in" – eye movement, facial expression, body language, voice inflection. However, determining when someone is intentionally lying versus trapped in self-deception or feeling guilty, or just forgetting or misunderstanding is very difficult to do. This is a big problem for professionals (e.g., judges, doctors, and teachers) who rely on knowing how to tell when someone is lying. This can be improved by reviewing a scene and watching a digital recording, or by having more than one person present at the time of questioning.

EXERCISE

Stand before a mirror and try to recreate the following expressions, and then describe these expressions as they appeared on your own face:

Happy	Surprised	Fearful
Sad	Angry	Disgusted

To meet someone face-to-face is to meet someone very personally and honestly. In the face of Christ we see the full glory of God (2 Cor. 4:6). **Jacob and Moses met God face-to-face** (Gen. 32:30; Ex. 33:11). As a result, Moses had to place a veil over his face as he walked among his people (Ex. 34:35). We read that Jesus' face shone like the sun (Matt. 17:2). Indeed, to have God's face shine upon us is a blessing (Ps. 80:3, 7), while to have God hide His face from us is a curse (Ps. 27:8-9; Isa. 64:7). The face of the Lord is against those who willfully sin (1 Pet. 3:12). Satan challenged God that Job would curse Him to His face (Job 1:11; Job 2:5),

> Write an Outline to Practice Speaking about *Standing Face to Face with God* using the following Bible verses:
>
> - Genesis 32:30
> - Exodus 33:11
> - Psalm 27:8-9
> - Psalm 80:3, 7
> - 1 Corinthians 13:12
> - 2 Corinthians 4:6
> - Revelation 22:4

An act of great respect and praise is to put your face to the ground – as an act of total submission and honor (Ruth 2:10; 1 Kings 1:23; Matt. 26:39). When Daniel interpreted King Nebuchadnezzar's dream, the king of Babylon fell on his face in great honor to Daniel and in humble recognition that Daniel's God was the God of all gods and King of all kings (Dan. 2:46). Someday we will see the face of our Lord without barriers or veils, but in true intimacy (1 Cor. 13:12; Rev. 22:4).

Daily Rhythms of the Body

> **EXAMPLE**
>
> The space station had its daily routine that kept all inhabitants on the same clock: They awoke at 7 AM; took part in easy warm-up stretching exercises at 9 AM; conducted computer-operated station checks at 10 AM. At 2 PM they performed an extensive exercise workout. At 7 PM they watched a movie, listened to music, or read a book. At 10 PM they were back in bed.

Your body has a "clock" – a circadian clock that is continually being adjusted by the solar cycles. In this cycling, body processes peak and ebb daily. At two in the morning you should be in your deepest sleep. At four in the morning your body should be at its lowest temperature. At seven at night you show your highest body temperature and blood pressure. This is why fever is more noticeable during the evening. In order to rest in the evening, you need to cool down. To wake up, you need to warm up. Therefore, you typically do not perform well after waking up, especially if woken up prematurely. Since airways constrict at night, exercise is harder in the early morning and breathing problems (e.g., asthma) are worse. At ten in the morning you should be most alert and at two in the afternoon, most physically coordinated. At three in the afternoon you should display your fastest reactions. At five in the afternoon you show your greatest physical endurance.

A day-night cycle of 24 hours or less seems to govern the body clock which affects hormones, heart rate, blood pressure, and body temperature. If you were in a cave, your body would still follow its body clock.

> ### EXAMPLE
>
> *I arrived in Brussels at 6 AM. I felt like sleeping but it was the start of a new day. By 10 AM I was in my hotel room. The bed looked so inviting! However, if I didn't adjust to the time change today I would be dead for my meeting tomorrow. So I put on my walking shoes and went out and around town, catching the sights. By 6 PM I was back in my room and ready for bed. I slept soundly through the night. The next day, after a cup of strong coffee, I was ready to negotiate.*

The body clock is advanced or delayed by changes in day-night cycles or changing time zones. Melatonin is a sleep hormone that is secreted in the evening and during sleep. People take melatonin to help them sleep or to adjust their body clock when changing time zones (offsetting jet lag). Adrenaline, however, speeds up your body clock – it makes a second seem to last for minutes. Thus, when you are very excited you remember details as if you had watched something happen in slow motion.

The effects of your body clock are offset or enhanced by other body activities. For example, a high carbohydrate meal promotes sleep while a high protein diet promotes alertness.

YOUR TURN

Finish the scene:

The FBI found Jacob in a cave up in the Blue Ridge. He had been living there for months. Candles lined the inner walls. Cans of food, plastic water bottles, and blankets were strewn across the floor. Now in prison, he seemed to stay on the regimen he must have kept when he lived in his cave . . .

7
Vision and Appearance

Zane Grey –
Wanderer of the Wasteland

The world in which he moved seemed transfigured, radiant with the last glow of dying day, with a glory of golden gleam. His heart pounded and his blood flooded to and fro, swelling his veins. Life on earth for him had been shot through and through with celestial fire. His feet were planted on the warm sands and his hands reached to touch the gray old boulders. He needed these to assure himself that he had not been turned into the soft, cool wind or the slanting amber rays so thickly glistening with particles of dust, or the great, soaring king of the eagles. Adam crushed a bunch of odorous sage to his face, smelled it, breathed it, tasted it; and the bitter sweetness thrilled his senses. It was real.

(New York: Grosset & Dunlap, 1923), 358

Understanding Vision

Vision is the processing of electromagnetic energy (light) by the excitation of pigments in the eye, which is converted to a nerve impulse transferred to the brain on the optic nerve . . . the more intense the light energy, the greater the excitation of pigments and the brighter the image. Your optic nerve is actually an extension of the brain – so yes, when someone looks deep into your eyes they are seeing your brain.

> EXAMPLE
>
> *"Did you see his eyes?"*
>
> *"No, I was watching his hands."*
>
> *"When he came running out of the apartment at the sound of the shot, his pupils were dilated. That means he was not in his office doing paperwork. He came from somewhere dark. Like the room where Jake was gunned down."*

The retina in your eyes consists of rods or black and white receptors to detect shades of gray; cones to detect color – three types for the primary colors of blue, green, and red. **To see color, you need sufficient light.** Thus at night you see shades of gray. Nocturnal animals are color-blind.

Although color-blindness or color deficiency occurs in humans, it rarely limits a person to seeing only black and white. **Common color blind-**

ness is the inability to see reds and greens – these colors appear as shades of blue and yellow. Traffic lights use the colors they do for "stop," "caution," and "go" so that color-blind people can still distinguish the signs.

Your eyes are continually adjusting to light. When light is bright or intense, your pupils constrict. When light is weak or dim, your pupils dilate. Dilation of pupils can also occur when you are excited or feeling attracted such as a man toward a woman. In the 1800s, some women took a drug called atropine or belladonna ("Beautiful Lady") to dilate their pupils to make them appear more attractive.

EXAMPLE

Upon examination of the body I found the woman had untreated cataracts. She had no peripheral vision and her ability to see at night had been very limited. So I went back over the scene of the accident. There was no way she could have seen the car coming at her without its headlights on as she crossed the street. The evidence presented in court was as cloudy as her vision.

Your eyes are well protected in several ways besides residing deep in your eye sockets. When you blink, your eyes are lubricated – thus you blink more often to protect your eyes from irritants such as dust, smoke, and allergens. You blink to wet your eyes when the air is dry or when air is being blown across your eyes. Your eyelashes protect against dirt and debris. Your eyebrows protect against sweat and water dropping down off your forehead. Thus, someone with faint or thin eyebrows would be more likely to wear a headband while working out or playing tennis.

Two eyes bring two slightly different images to your brain for image processing. Your eyes allow you to see peripherally and to judge depth in three-dimensions. **Far-sighted** people can see objects far off, but objects close by are fuzzy. Long-term damage from ultraviolet (UV) light can contribute to the far-sighted condition. Sunglasses with UV protection help protect your eyes from UV light. **Near-sighted** people can see close up objects, but objects far off are fuzzy. People who do a lot of close-up work with their eyes are more prone to becoming near-sighted. Corrective lenses, known as eyeglasses, or contact lenses can minimize most eye problems.

Eye injuries or accidents are the more common causes of a loss of vision in one eye.

Images are focused onto the retina by your cornea and lens. Your brain then has to flip the picture 180 degrees in order to interpret it. But as you age the lenses harden and become thicker, so that you lose focus and color vision, and you may develop cataracts (partial blindness). **With age your pupil shrinks and the reduction in light sensors reduces your ability to see in the dark.** Also, you have more trouble adjusting to light intensity (such as when coming out of a movie theatre into broad daylight).

People can be totally blind or legally blind. Someone who is legally blind or visually impaired has a significant deficiency in seeing objects at a distance and/or seeing objects peripherally. This can come from cataracts or glaucoma. In poverty-stricken areas of the world and undeveloped countries, blindness caused by parasites and diseases can be endemic.

EXERCISE

At nighttime, describe your bed room with all the lights on. Pretend you are describing it to a person who cannot see. Then turn the lights off so that it is as dark as you can make it. After 15 minutes, to let your eyes adjust to the darkness, describe your room aloud. When you turn back on the lights, compare the descriptions that you wrote when the lights were on to your verbal description when the lights were turned off.

Light of the World

God created night and day, light and dark, morning and evening. He contrasts light and darkness to make spiritual truth come alive to us. The Bible tells us that God sees (2 Kings 19:16; Job 34:21-22) and does not miss the acts of the wicked (Gen. 38:7; 2 Kings 17:18) but gives favor to those whom He sees will follow His ways (Gen. 6:8; 18:3; 19:19; 39:4; Ps. 34:15). It is God's plan that we lift up our eyes to Him with praise (Ps. 123:1-2). We can plead to God to hear and see our prayers and praise, as well as to see and punish those who hate the Lord and His people (Isa. 37:14-17). Yet we are to keep our eyes open, as watchmen ready to warn others of the dangers of sin (Ezek. 33:6). While God gave His people the eyes to witness His work on earth, such as their freedom from Egypt and slavery, God still had to give them the eyes that see and ears that hear spiritual truth.

When Adam and Eve's eyes were opened to good and evil (Gen. 3:5), **sin came into the world.** One day, however, there will be no more tears in our eyes (Rev. 21:4). In the meantime, Jesus brings healing to the blind (Matt. 9:30; Luke 7:21;18:42-43). Blessings bring about good vision, while sin leads to blindness (Matt. 13:15-16; Mark 8:18).

God has always allowed us to see His work and blessings throughout history (Deut. 3:21;11:7). The Word of God came at times in a vision (Gen. 15:1; 1 Sam. 3:1; Acts 16:9;18:9; Rev. 9:17). Jesus appeared to His disciples in full sight after He arose from the dead (Luke 24:30-32). It was important that they saw Him again with their eyes. The appearance of Jesus in all His glory is described in the Bible as being adorned in a white robe, shining as light with a face like the sun (Matt. 17:3; Mark 16:5; Acts 10:30-31). And someday we will join Him and He will dress us in white and place on our heads a crown (Rev. 3:5, 4:4, and 19:14).

Jesus is the light of the world, and we are to reflect that light like a lamp upon a table. Light eradicates darkness. Light brings forth truth and hope. Light reveals what is unseen in darkness, bringing about repentance or bringing about judgment. Vision is one way to seek the truth, to stay out of danger, to guide others, and to praise the Lord by the beauty of the creation which is His handiwork. The Bible is rich in its use of the sense of sight to bring out many important insights.

Write an Outline to Practice Speaking about *The Eyes of God* using the following Bible verses:

- Genesis 6:8
- Genesis 18:3
- Genesis 38:7
- Genesis 39:4
- 2 Kings 19:16
- Job 34:21-22
- Psalm 34:15
- Isaiah 37:14-17

Describing Eyes and Hair

The type and level of pigments in your eyes determine the color of your eyes. Your natural eye color is genetically determined by the time you are one year old even though your eye color at birth might have been blue. You inherit genes for brown, green, or blue eyes, with these colors ranging from dark brown to light blue. Since you inherit eye color from your parents, there are ways to predict to some extent which eye color you will have or which eye color you will likely not have. As with hair color, the two types of pigments that determine eye color are eumelanin and pheomelanin. However, depending on environmental lighting, the color shade of one's eyes will vary.

The most common eye colors are brown, light brown, green, gray, and blue. Brown is the most common eye color worldwide. Green and gray are the rarest eye colors. Other colors include: whiskey eyes (light brown), hazel (yellowish brown), amber (golden-coppery) or "cat eyes," steel blue-gray, and violet. People can have two different colored eyes or irises such as blue and hazel, or blue and green.

EXAMPLE

The soldier returned after the war only to find that the mother of his child had died of typhoid fever and his daughter was at the orphanage. They lined up the children of approximate same age. Nine had black hair and brown eyes. One with black hair had hazel eyes. He looked more closely. He handed her a shiny coin. She smiled and her dimples came forth like fireworks – it was her! This was the child he had come back to find – to reclaim as his own.

Hair color and eye color and skin tone often show associations, such as with blue-eyed, blonde haired Scandinavians. Brown hair and green eyes might be Celtic in origin. Black hair and brown eyes would be common in peoples of African and Asian descent. Red hair is more typically associated with peoples of the British Isles.

EXAMPLE

I thought she was a twin sister. Except for darkened hair and green eyes, she looked identical. The green eyes were captivating. Since I had not yet asked her sister for a date, I thought I could begin here – with her twin. So I eased over to say hello. As soon as she spoke, I almost fell flat on my face. She wasn't a twin – she was wearing contacts.

Contact lenses can do more than correct vision, they can change the color of your eyes. Lenses can enhance your eye color (make a lightly colored eye more intense), or change the color to hazel, green, blue, violet, amethyst, or gray.

The color of hair also comes from a mixture of the pigments eumelanin and pheomelanin. The greater the melanin (the brown and black pigment), the darker the hair color. The greater the pheomelanin (the yellow and red pigment), the lighter the hair color. Hair color varies from a pale yellow or blonde to a deep black. Within each color the shades can vary from person to person, and even for one person over time (such as with age). Hair that is bleached will appear yellow.

Natural hair color is typically either blonde, brown, red, or black with black being the most common overall. This is determined by genetics or ethnicity, which also determines skin tone and eye color. Thus, you have a natural hair color and you have a corresponding skin tone and eye color. Black and brown hair colors are common worldwide, although texture may change.

Hair texture is described by its thickness, elasticity, and strength. **Hair can be fine or coarse, thick, or thin, straight, or wooly.** Blonde hair is less common whereas red hair is becoming rare. Other types of hair colors include: auburn, brunette, chestnut, cinnamon, dirty blonde, fair, jet black, platinum blonde, raven, sandy, salt and pepper, silver, and strawberry blonde.

Levels of hair color follow a scale based on natural hair colors:
1. **Black**
2. Very dark brown
3. Dark brown
4. **Brown**
5. Medium brown
6. Light brown
7. Light brown
8. Dark **blonde**
9. Light blonde
10. Very light blonde
11. Light platinum blonde

> **EXAMPLE**
>
> *I checked the various photos the police provided me. We tried to piece together her disguised features – so that we could find her in the high school yearbook. One photo had her with black colored hair. In another she had platinum hair. In another, red hair. Considering that she had freckles, and always used a Celtic name, we looked for the girls with red hair. That is how we found her.*

As you age, the cells that produce pigment die off and your hair loses its color. As a result, gray hair grows in, and can give way to white hair. The timing is largely a genetic factor – some people gray early in life. Hair color can also change after a person dies. In fact, brown and black pigments degrade faster with time such that a dead person's hair will become redder in color.

> **EXAMPLE**
>
> *When the police pulled the lady's body from the marsh I did not recognize her – I remembered her with deep black-colored, thick hair. This woman had thin hair of a reddish color.*

You can have your hair colored with a permanent or temporary hair coloring. A "color wheel," as artists would use to mix paints, guides the desired mix between your natural hair color and new hair color. Thus, if a group of girls wanted to obtain red hair, but they had different natural hair colors, the color treatments would vary from one to the next.

EXERCISE

Look in the mirror and write a description of your face including eye color and hair. Then switch the color of your eyes and hair to make five different descriptions. Share the descriptions with a friend. Ask your friend which of the following best fits the facial descriptions you wrote:

– Friendly and open

– Shy and reserved

– Confident and strong willed

– Unsure and fearful

Skin Color

Skin color is more varied than white, black, or yellow (Caucasian, African, or Asian). There are three dozen or more possible color tones. These can be found on a skin tone chart (black, dark brown, light brown, tan, reddish brown, yellow, pinkish, white) and each varies from pale to dark. Historically, the further away one lived from the equator the lighter would be one's skin color. However, with greater movement of people around the world, this trend in skin color has become quite variable.

> **EXAMPLE**
>
> Amid the painful movement of disheveled homeless victims in the food line in the hot afternoon sun, walked a man of small stature with blonde hair and dark skin. His hands were weathered and his skin leathery. It had been months since he had tasted fish soup and his taste buds ached for home cooking. But today was Wednesday, and he would have to settle for sloppy joe and beans.

Skin color at birth is basically determined by your genetic makeup, although local climate and long-term exposure to sunlight and other factors (e.g., one's health, skin quality) alter your original tone. Each person is unique. Your genetic makeup determines your blend of skin pigments or melanin (pheomelanin and eumelanin).

Melanin is a natural sunscreen for the skin. The more exposure to ultraviolet radiation (direct sunlight) the more melanin your skin will produce. When you tan by the sun your skin turns a darker tone. Lighter skin favors more absorption of ultraviolet radiation, thus lighter skinned people tend to sunburn more easily.

Ultraviolet radiation triggers the body's production of vitamin D, which is very important for the development of healthy bones. Dark skin reduces vitamin D production. Since people living near the equator tend to get a lot of exposure to sunlight and have more than enough vitamin D, their bodies take on darker skins since they do not need to overproduce vitamin D. People who live closer to the North and South poles tend to be lighter skinned to maximize absorption of sunlight to produce vitamin D to stay healthy. However, some people obtain vitamin D from other sources such as fish, and even though they live closer to the poles they have darker skin because their bodies have sufficient vitamin D through their diet. In general, women tend to be lighter in skin tone than men and this may be because they have a greater need for vitamin D.

YOUR TURN

Finish the scene:

There was chaos everywhere. I stood on the end of the pier looking back at the bodies lying down, kneeling, and sitting. How did a dozen grow to about thirty victims in ten minutes? The sun beat down as I adjusted my hat. It was 3 PM – time to go to work. In that mess of bodies were people who were faking it. I opened the gate and walked between the roller coaster and the shaker, observing . . .

Where to Watch People

God instructed men and women about their appearance to each other (Deut. 22:5) and that clothing could carry diseases (Lev. 13:47). Much could be determined by how a person dressed. Wealthy people or people of a king's household wore clothes of fine linen of many colors, especially the colors purple, blue, and white (2 Sam. 13:18; Esther 8:15; Dan. 5:7, 16). Sackcloth was a coarse, dark colored cloth – perhaps of goat hair – used to make bags as well as to be worn without undergarments, close to the skin, when mourning and grieving. Many people in the Bible tore their clothes and put on sackcloth to weep and wail and mourn deeply (Gen. 37:34; 2 Kings 19:1; Ps. 69:10-11; Esther 4:1).

Public transportation is one place to observe people of all ages, races, income levels, and backgrounds. People appear as couples, in groups, and alone. People appear dressed up or dressed quite shabbily. You can also observe how people interact socially. There are students, people going to and coming from work, retired folks, and people going to and coming from hospitals or church. People are in different dress depending on the seasons of the year, and depending on the weather.

In order to observe people, check out the bus, subway, or elevated train at different times of the day: Rush hour; 10-12 AM, 1-3 PM, and 8-10 PM. You might see people looking for jobs or returning from the hospital or the welfare office during the midday periods. At 7-8 AM and 3-4 PM you might find students of all ages. Late at night you might observe shift workers.

> Write an Outline to Practice Speaking about *How God Appears to Me* using the following Bible verses:
>
> - Genesis 12:7
> - Numbers 20:6
> - Deuteronomy 31:15
> - 2 Chronicles 7:12
> - Daniel 8:15
> - Daniel 10:18
> - Matthew 1:20
> - Mark 16:9
> - Mark 16:14
> - Luke 24:37-40

Prepare some forms for recording your observations before you take the trip on public transportation. On the forms put:

Type of people observed (family, students, elderly, etc.);
- Style of outer wear;
- Time of year;
- Time of day;
- Body language displayed;
- Social interactions displayed;
- Unique observations.

The information you collect on these forms can help you describe similar people in other public situations such as at the mall, in the park, or on the avenue.

God tells us that He does not judge as we do by physical appearances (1 Sam. 16:7; John 7:24), and thus He chose David to be king above his brothers. Appearances can be misleading, as with a false prophet in sheep's clothing (Matt. 7:15). Adam and Eve enjoyed no shame in being naked (Gen. 2:25) until their eyes were opened (Gen. 3:7), after which God fashioned garments for them (Gen. 3:21). Thus, we appear to each other today in a fallen or sinful state. But coming is the day when God will clothe us in glory (Rev. 3:5).

Writer's Observations

Setting: Bus   Date: June 12

Time of Day: 10 AM – 12 noon   Type of Day: Sunny, 80s

People Observed	Outer Wear	Body Language	Social Interactions	Other Observations
Male teenagers	Printed T-shirts, knee-length baggy shorts, sneakers, no jewelry, no hats, short haircuts	Confident Macho Loud	Joking with each other; no interaction with other people; sit in their group	Conversation was about girls, music, and friends
Man about 65 years old	Buttoned shirt, dress pants, dress shoes, clean shaven	Confident Polite Predictable	Quiet, thanked the bus driver; said hello to a lady; smiled at a child	Showed interest in other people on the bus but annoyance at the group of teenagers making noise.

Chapter Notes

Chapter 1

Just Imagine
Conduct a Bible study using a concordance that matches the Bible version in your possession. Search the Bible using the words from the chapters and sections of this book.

More Than Five Senses
Internet searches can provide interesting links to information on the senses, such as searching for items on the "human senses," although many sites still limit the discussion to the five more common senses. A site that provides state-of-the-art findings on the human senses is www.monell.org, for the Monell Chemical Senses Center in Philadelphia.

When giving a character a disease, injury, or disorder, study the effects of the disease or its treatment, such as side effects of drugs on the sensory system. One web site to check is www.sensory-processing-disorder.com and another site is www.nidcd.nih.gov/health/smelltaste.

Help for Writers and Speakers
Internet searches can uncover more detailed information on each sense. Use the sensory system's name for the search.

Chapter 2

Taste, Flavor and Aroma
The Smell and Taste Center in Philadelphia has interesting information on these senses from a medical perspective, and can be found at www.med.upenn.edu/stc.

To obtain more information on flavor with regards to foods and beverages, search the Internet using such key words as "flavor," "aroma," or "tea," "coffee," "chocolate," and "perfume." One site of interest for wine is www.aromadictionary.com.

The Nose and Tongue

Conduct a concordance-based search of the Bible and the Internet using the words "nose" and "tongue."

Sweet, Salty, Sour, and Bitter

For more information search for Internet sites on "chocolate," "caffeine," "cocoa," and "sugar."

Taste and Discernment

Conduct a concordance-based search of the Bible using the word "taste."

A Pleasing Aroma

G.D. Armerding's *The Fragrance of the Lord: Toward a Deeper Appreciation of the Bible* (New York: Harper and Row Publishers, Inc., 1979) provides some additional reading as does A. Gilbert's *What the Nose Knows – The Science of Scent in Everyday Life* (New York: Crown Publishers, 2008).

Chapter 3

Perfume

For more information go to www.aftelier.com or www.essentialoils.org. For more information see Diane Ackerman's book *A Natural History of the Senses* (New York: Vantage Books, 1995). Also see Mandy Aftel's book *Essence and Alchemy: A Natural History of Perfume* (New York: North Point Press, 2001).

To research the scents of particular perfumes go to www.basenotes.net and search under Fragrance Directory. Here you will find listings of the top notes (such as ylang-ylang), middle notes (such as rose), and base notes (such as sandalwood) for specific perfumes. A perfume aroma or fragrance wheel can also be found on the Internet.

Emotion-evoking Aromas

For more information see Diane Ackerman's book *A Natural History of the Senses* (New York: Vantage Books, 1995) and Avery Gilbert's book *What the Nose Knows* (New York: Crown Publishers, 2008). For a library of essential oils, the plants they come from, and odor characteristics, visit www.bojensen.net. For a variety of supplies and materials including smell test strips, search the Internet using keywords "aromatherapy" and "essential oils."

Smell of Death, Disease, and Sin

For more information see B. Gibbons, "The Intimate Sense of Smell" (*National Geographic Society Magazine* 170:3:324-360) and Diane Ackerman's book *A Natural History of the Senses* (New York: Vantage Books, 1995) and Avery Gilbert's book *What the Nose Knows* (New York: Crown Publishers, 2008).

The Anointed One

G.D. Armerding's *The Fragrance of the Lord: Toward a Deeper Appreciation of the Bible*. (New York: Harper and Row Publishers, Inc., 1979) provides some additional reading.

Environmental Fragrancing

For more information search the Internet for actual companies that provide a market for fragrances. New products appear almost monthly.

Incense is Something Burned

You can search the Internet for "essential oils," and "aromatherapy" to find many sources of ingredients that you can actually purchase and try smelling firsthand.

Clothing and Building Materials

Conduct a concordance-based search of the Bible using the words "clothing," "sackcloth," "linen," "wood," and "temple." Also, visit a lumber yard or home supply center to smell and touch different woods (cedar, mahogany, pine, etc.).

Chapter 4

A Sip of Water

For some interesting information on the latest trend in bottled waters and water tasting, search the Internet for "bottled water" and "drinking water." One site of interest is www.finewaters.com.

Coffee's Aroma

There are many books on coffee brewing and blending that are easy to find in the library. For more information you can search the Internet where you can find the "coffee flavor wheel" at various sites. One Internet site is www.sweetmarias.com. For historical background on coffee and its influence see T. Standage's *A History of the World in 6 Glasses* (New York: Walker and Company, 2005).

The Lure of Spices

You can search the Internet for "herbs and spices" to find many sources of ingredients that you can actually purchase and try smelling firsthand. One fascinating web site is www.bojensen.net, which has pictures and descriptions of the trees and plants from which essential oils are obtained.

Additional reading includes G.D. Armerding's *The Fragrance of the Lord: Toward a Deeper Appreciation of the Bible* (New York: Harper and Row Publishers, Inc., 1979) and R. L. Doty's (ed.) "Introduction and Historical Perspective" in *Handbook of Olfaction and Gustation* (New York: Marcel Dekker, Inc., 1995) and D. Hocking and C. Hocking's *Romantic Lovers* (Eugene, OR: Harvest House Publishers, 1986).

Time for Tea

For more information search the Internet using the word "tea" and search for tea producers' web sites such as www.ineeka.com and the Tea Association of the USA at www.teausa.org. For historical background on tea and its influence see T. Standage's *A History of the World in 6 Glasses* (New York: Walker and Company, 2005).

The Bouquet of Wine

For more information consult: http://wineserver.ucdavis.edu; www.winearomawheel.com; and www.winepros.org. For an historical background on wine and its influence on history see T. Standage's *A His-*

tory of the World in 6 Glasses (New York: Walker and Company, 2005).

The Body of a Good Beer
For more information, go to http://brewingtechniques.com and www.alabev.com/taste.htm. For historical background on beer and its influence see T. Standage's *A History of the World in 6 Glasses* (New York: Walker and Company, 2005).

Off Flavors in Fish
Search the Internet for "fish flavors" and borrow a student chef's textbook on food and cooking.

There will be a Feast
Conduct a concordance-based search of the Bible on the word "feast."

Chapter 5

Understanding Audition
For more information search the Internet using words such as "hearing," the "ear," and "sound."

Faith Comes by Hearing
Conduct a concordance-based search of the Bible using the words "ears," "hearing," "voice," and "speak."

The Ear and Body Balance
For more information on the ear and body balance search the Internet using words such as "ear," "inner ear," and "body balance."

Where to Find Sounds of Life
Other likely places to record sounds include City Hall and the indoor shopping mall.

Help in Describing Sounds
For more information conduct a word search using dictionary software or simply thumb through that old, dusty dictionary on your shelf.

Chapter 6

Touch is Very Important
Much information can be found in college textbooks as well as by searching the Internet for sensory terms including "touch."

Pain is Quite Complex
There are medical and psychological college textbooks that address pain. For more information see "The Changing Science of Pain" by Mary Carmichael in *Newsweek* magazine (June 4, 2007; pp. 40-45). Also, for more information go to The American Pain Foundation at www.painfoundation.org or the American Pain Society at www.ampainsoc.org or the National Headache Foundation at www.headaches.org.

Healing Powers
One book that highlights the observations a good physician makes when examining a patient is Dr. J. Groopman's *How Doctors Think* (New York: First Mariner Books, 2008).

Body Tremors
For more information refer to the Essential Tremor Foundation at www.essentialtremor.org.

Facial Expressions
For more information refer to J. Cole's book *About Face* (Cambridge, MA: The MIT Press, 1999). For more information search the Internet for "facial expressions." There are many different charts available on facial expressions and some web sites or software with animated facial expressions that are used by actors. There are resources for actors that are quite developed for studying and copying facial expressions. These use real people or cartoons to develop a facial repertoire. An excellent resource is found at www.paulekman.com where the work of Dr. Paul Ekman can be accessed.

Daily Rhythms of the Body
For more information see K. Wright, "Time of Our Lives" in *Scientific American* (Feb., 2006; 287:3:58-65). Also see the book by J.M. Water-

house, D.S. Minors, M.E. Waterhouse, T. Reilly, and G. Atkinson, *Keeping in Time with Your Body Clock* (New York: Oxford University Press, Inc., 2002).

Chapter 7

Understanding Vision
Much information can be found on the Internet by searching for "vision."

Light of the World
Conduct a concordance-based search of the Bible using the words "light," "darkness," "shine," and "lamp."

Describing Eyes and Hair
Web sites to help a writer make decisions about the types, style, and color of a character's eyes are numerous – just search the Internet using the key words "eye color." You can determine what eye color a child might have based on her parents. There are charts to determine this on the Internet.

There are sites on the Internet that can help a writer make decisions about the types, style, and color of a character's hair – just search the Internet using the key words "hair color" or "hair style." You can search for the latest trends and styles, learn about the chemistry of hair color, and choose hair colors. You can also borrow magazines from your hair stylist.

Skin Color
For more information, search the Internet using key words "skin tone" or "skin color." You will find scientific and medical studies, skin health product information, and skin tone charts for photographers and artists.

Where to Watch People
Other places to watch people include the public square or park, the indoor shopping mall, and the library.

Index

Aaron, 92, 95
Ackerman, Diane, 23
Adam, 46, 143, 175, 199, 210
Aloe, 96
Anoint, 17, 83, 84, 96, 112
    garments, 17, 95, 112
Anointing oil, 17, 70, 83, 95, 96
Anosmia, 41, 58, 132
Aroma, 39, 40, 59, 60, 67, 69, 74, 80, 91, 95, 107, 112, 119, 121, 131
    sweet, 49, 59
Appearance, 23, 123, 124, 199, 209
    sackcloth, 209
Aromatherapy, 73, 75, 84
Aromatic oils, 74
Audition, 26, 139

Balance, 22, 26, 135, 145, 146
Balm, 17, 84
    of Gilead, 85
Barzillai, 59
Beer, 123-125
Bitter, 19, 26, 39, 40, 49, 51, 52, 57, 58, 80, 93, 104, 108, 117, 124
    poisons, 52, 80
Blood, taste of, 19, 79
Body clock, 186
Bradbury, Ray, 101
Bread, symbolism of, 19, 132
Breath, of life, 46
Building materials, 95

Cadaverine, 78-79
Caffeine, 40, 107, 115, 116, 185

Cedar, 17, 70, 95, 96
Church, 17, 132
Chocolate, 52
Christ, 17, 19, 59, 80, 131, 183
    aroma of, 19, 59, 60, 65, 83, 93, 112, 131
    offerings to, 59, 92, 112
Clothing, scented, 97
Coffee, 49, 107-110
Cold, symbolism of, 57, 166
Communion, 18, 19, 132

Daniel, 184
David, 83, 210
Deacon, 17-18
Deaf, 143, 175
Dickens, Charles, 37
Discernment, 57, 58, 132

Ears, 21, 26, 80, 139, 140, 145, 175, 199
Eden, Garden of, 19, 96, 132, 143, 175
Esau, 51, 95
Exteroception, 21
Eyes, 21, 22, 26, 80, 181, 195-197, 201, 202, 210

Feelings, sensory, 40
Finger, of God, 175
Fish, 78, 127-128, 206
Face, 181-184
    of Christ, 199
Facial Coding System, 182
Flavor, 25, 39-40, 49, 53, 57, 131
Fragrancing, environmental, 87
Frankincense, 17, 67, 68, 70, 74, 92, 93, 112

Galbanum, 17, 68, 92
Gall, 52
Grey, Zane, 193
Guide: to sensory systems, 26; for speakers, 27; for writers, 31-32

Hair, 69, 70, 78, 84, 165, 201-204

Headaches, 73, 170
Healing, 84, 112, 143, 175, 199
Hearing, 21, 22, 23, 26, 60, 131, 140, 143
Hell, 80
Holy Spirit, 83
Hot, symbolism of, 57, 79, 166

Incense, 17, 49, 83, 91-93
Interoception, 21

Jacob, 83, 95, 183
Jesus, 17-19, 23, 52, 54, 57, 59, 80, 83, 84, 96, 127, 131, 143, 175, 183, 199, 200
Jonah, 79

Kiss, 176

Lazarus, 80, 84
Light, 131, 195, 196-197, 199-200
Lot, 53

Malodors, 88
Mary, 84
Melanin, 202, 205, 206
Melatonin, 88
Miracle fruit, 57
Myrrh, 17, 52, 67, 70, 95, 96, 111-112

Naomi, 52
Nicodemus, 96
Nose, 21, 26, 40-41, 45-46, 67, 131, 145, 166

Odor, 40-42, 59, 60, 73, 78, 79
Offerings, 19, 59, 92
Ointment, 70, 84
Olive oil, 17, 84
Onycha, 92

Pain, 21, 26, 39, 51, 80, 165, 169-173
    words of, 172-173
Paradise tree, 96

Passover, 19, 51, 132
Perfume, 59, 67-70, 79, 84, 93, 96, 112
Pomade, 70
Proprioception, 22, 25
Putrescine, 79

Salty, 26, 39, 49, 104
Senses, 26
   adaptation of, 22
   cold, 26, 39, 166, 177
   cutaneous, 21
   hot, 26, 39, 40, 165, 166
   kinesthetic, 21, 22, 26
   vestibular, 21, 22, 26
Smell, 21, 23, 25, 26, 28, 39, 40, 41-42, 59, 67, 78, 132, 176
   and God, 46, 59, 79, 80, 95, 131
   of death, 77-80
Solomon, 70, 91
Somatosensory system, 21
Sound, 22, 26, 139-140, 149-150
   words of, 153-155
Sour, 26, 39, 40, 57
   symbolism of, 19, 53-54
Spices, 67, 69, 70, 83, 92, 111
   cassia, 17, 95, 112
   cinnamon, 67, 69, 70, 108, 112, 115, 117
   coriander, 67, 111
   cumin, 83, 111
   hyssop, 52, 74, 112
   rue, 112
   saffron, 70, 112
Spikenard, 17, 70, 84, 112
Shittim wood, 96
Skin, 69, 70, 74, 78, 96, 112, 202, 205-206
   and senses, 21, 26, 80, 165-166
St. Paul, 65
Steinbeck, John, 137
Sweet, 26, 39, 49-50, 58
   symbolism of, 19, 23, 46, 49, 53-54, 58, 59, 65, 92
Synesthesia, 22, 142

Tactile sense, 22, 26, 165, 166
Tasseography, 109
Taste, 21, 25, 26, 39-40, 49, 50, 57, 80, 131
    symbolism of, 19, 57, 131-132
Tea, 77, 109, 115-118, 121
Tolkien, J.R.R., 163
Tongue, 26, 39, 45, 47, 49, 165
Touch, 19, 21, 22, 25, 26, 131, 165-166, 175, 176
    and God, 23, 131, 175
Tremors, 177-178

Umami, 26, 40

Vision, 21, 23, 26, 171, 195-197, 202
    symbolism of, 131, 199, 200
Voice, of God, 143

Water, 103-106, 109, 115, 119, 127
    and God, 19, 52, 57
Wine, 57, 78, 109, 119-122
    symbolism of, 18, 19, 52, 54, 57, 95, 132
Wormwood, 80

RESOURCES FROM HEALTHY LIFE PRESS

Unless otherwise noted on the site itself, shipping is free for all products purchased through www.healthylifepress.com.

NEW RELEASES – FALL 2014

Mommy, What's 'Died' Mean? - How the Butterfly Story Helped Little Dave Understand His Grandpa's Death, by Linda Swain Gill; Illustrated by David Lee Bass (a.k.a. "Little Dave") – Designed to assist Christian parents and other adults who love and care about children to talk with them about the difficult subject of death, the story traces a small child's experience following his grandpa's and shows how his mother sensitively answered his questions about death by using simple examples derived from the birth of a butterfly. Little Dave's story is colorfully illustrated and designed for a child and parent or trusted adult to read together. The story has been created especially for children from pre-kindergarten through 4th grade. Discussion questions are included for each story page to help determine how much the child understands. A simple imitation game is also included to help involve the child in the story. Several pages at the end of the book contain suggestions about how to discuss death and dying with children of various ages. (**Full-color printed book:** $14.99; PDF eBook: $9.99; both together: $19.99 – direct from publisher; printed books and eBooks available at *www.Amazon.com*; *www.BN.com*; *www.deepershopping.com*, and wherever books are sold.)

No Worries - Spiritual and Mental Health Counseling for Anxiety, by Elaine Leong Eng, MD – Offering a unique spiritual and mental health perspective on a major malady of our age, this practicing Christian psychiatrist has packed a dose of reality mixed with medicine and faith into a book aimed at informing, inspiring, and equipping those who wish to better help those who struggle with anxiety and related disorders, both inside and outside the church. As one endorser said, "I travel all over the world. I see fellow believers suffering from different forms of anxiety and worry. Dr. Eng's book gives me tools to recognize when people are suffering and how to encourage them to get the help they need." (Printed book: $19.99; PDF eBook: $9.99; both together: $24.99 – direct from publisher; printed books and eBooks available at *www.Amazon.com*; *www.BN.com*; *www.deepershopping.com*, and wherever books are sold.)

If God Is So Good, Why Do I Hurt So Bad?, by David B. Biebel, DMin – This **25th Anniversary Edition** of a best-selling classic (over 200,000 copies in print worldwide, in a dozen languages) is the book's first major revision since its initial release in 1989. This new version features additional original material related to the conundrum of suffering and faith (with principles learned along the way), and chapter ending questions for personal or group use. Endorser Sheila Walsh wrote, "I believe this is one of the most profound, empathetic and beautiful books ever written on the subject of suffering and loss. There is no attempt to quickly ease our pain but rather, with an understanding born in the crucible God uniquely designed for him, David offers a place to stand, a place to fall and a place to rise again. This book left an indelible mark on my heart over twenty years ago and now with this new release the gift is fresh and fragrant. I highly commend this to you!" (Printed book: $14.99; PDF eBook: $9.99; both together: $19.95 – direct from publisher; printed books and eBooks available at *www.Amazon.com*; *www.BN.com*; *www.deepershopping.com*, and wherever books are sold.)

Earlier Releases

We've Got Mail: The New Testament Letters in Modern English – As Relevant Today as Ever! by Rev. Warren C. Biebel, Jr. – A modern English paraphrase of the New Testament Letters, sure to inspire in readers a loving appreciation for God's Word. (Printed book: $9.95; PDF eBook: $6.95; both together: $15.00 – direct from publisher; printed books and eBooks available at *www.Amazon.com*; *www.BN.com*; *www.deepershopping.com*, and wherever books are sold.)

 **Hearth & Home – Recipes for Life**, by Karey Swan (7th Edition) – Far more than a cookbook, this classic is a life book, with recipes for life as well as for great food. Karey describes how to buy and prepare from scratch a wide variety of tantalizing dishes, while weaving into the book's fabric the wisdom of the ages plus the recipe that she and her husband used to raise their kids. A great gift for Christmas or for a new bride. (Perfect Bound book [8 x 10, glossy cover]: $17.95; PDF eBook: $12.95; both together: $24.95 – direct from publisher; printed books and eBooks available at www.Amazon.com; www.BN.com; www.deepershopping.com, and wherever books are sold.)

Who Me, Pray? Prayer 101: Praying Aloud, for Beginners, by Gary A. Burlingame – Who Me, Pray? is a practical guide for prayer, based on Jesus' direction in "The Lord's Prayer," with examples provided for use in typical situations where you might be asked or expected to pray in public. (Printed book: $6.95; PDF eBook: $2.99; both together: $7.95 – direct from publisher; printed books and eBooks available at www.Amazon.com; www.BN.com; www.deepershopping.com, and wherever books are sold.)

 **My Broken Heart Sings**, the poetry of Gary Burlingame – In 1987, Gary and his wife Debbie lost their son Christopher John, at only six months of age, to a chronic lung disease. This life-changing experience gave them a special heart for helping others through similar loss and pain. (Printed book: $10.95; PDF eBook: $6.95; both together: $13.95 – direct from publisher; printed books and eBooks available at www.Amazon.com; www. BN.com; www.deepershopping.com, and wherever books are sold.)

After Normal: One Teen's Journey Following Her Brother's Death, by Diane Aggen – Based on a journal the author kept following her younger brother's death. It offers helpful insights and understanding for teens facing a similar loss or for those who might wish to understand and help teens facing a similar loss. (Printed book: $11.95; PDF eBook: $6.95; both together: $15.00 – direct from publisher; printed books and eBooks

available at *www.Amazon.com*; *www.BN.com*; *www.deepershopping.com*, and wherever books are sold.)

In the Unlikely Event of a Water Landing – Lessons Learned from Landing in the Hudson River, by Andrew Jamison, MD – The author was flying standby on US Airways Flight 1549 toward Charlotte on January 15, 2009, from New York City, where he had been interviewing for a residency position. Little did he know that the next stop would be the Hudson River. Riveting and inspirational, this book would be especially helpful for people in need of hope and encouragement. (Printed book: $8.95; PDF eBook: $6.95; both together: $12.95 – direct from publisher; printed books and eBooks available at *www.Amazon.com*; *www.BN.com*; *www.deepershopping.com*, and wherever books are sold.)

Finding Martians in the Dark – Everything I Needed to Know About Teaching Took Me Only 30 Years to Learn, by Dan M. Biebel – Packed with wise advice based on hard experience, and laced with humor, this book is a perfect teacher's gift year-round. Susan J. Wegmann, PhD, says, "Biebel's sardonic wit is mellowed by a genuine love for kids and teaching. . . . A Whitman-like sensibility flows through his stories of teaching, learning, and life." (Printed book: $10.95; PDF eBook: $6.95; Together: $15.00 – direct from publisher; printed books and eBooks available at *www.Amazon.com*; *www.BN.com*; *www.deepershopping.com*, and wherever books are sold.)

Because We're Family and **Because We're Friends,** by Gary A. Burlingame – Sometimes things related to faith can be hard to discuss with your family and friends. These booklets are designed to be given as gifts, to help you open the door to discussing spiritual matters with family members and friends who are open to such a conversation. (Printed book: $5.95 each; PDF eBook: $4.95 each; both together: $9.95 [printed & eBook of the same title] – direct from publisher; printed books and eBooks available at *www.Amazon.com*; *www.BN.com*; *www.deepershopping.com*, and wherever books are sold.)

The Transforming Power of Story: How Telling Your Story Brings Hope to Others and Healing to Yourself, by Elaine Leong Eng, MD, and David B. Biebel, DMin – This book demonstrates, through multiple true life stories, how sharing one's story, especially in a group setting, can bring hope to listeners and healing to the one who shares. Individuals facing difficulties will find this book greatly encouraging. (Printed book: $14.99; PDF eBook: $9.99; both together: $19.99 – direct from publisher; printed books and eBooks available at *www.Amazon.com*; *www.BN.com*; *www.deepershopping.com*, and wherever books are sold.)

You Deserved a Better Father: Good Parenting Takes a Plan, by Robb Brandt, MD – About parenting by intention, and other lessons the author learned through the loss of his firstborn son. It is especially for parents who believe that bits and pieces of leftover time will be enough for their own children. (Printed book: $12.95 each; PDF eBook: $6.95; both together: $17.95 – direct from publisher; printed books and eBooks available at *www.Amazon.com*; *www.BN.com*; *www.deepershopping.com*, and wherever books are sold.)

Printed Cover   eBook Cover

Jonathan, You Left Too Soon, by David B. Biebel, DMin – One pastor's journey through the loss of his son, into the darkness of depression, and back into the light of joy again, emerging with a renewed sense of mission. (Printed book: $12.95; PDF eBook: $5.99; both together: $15.00 – direct from publisher; printed books and eBooks available at *www.Amazon.com*; *www.BN.com*; *www.deepershopping.com*, and wherever books are sold.)

Unless otherwise noted on the site itself, shipping is free for all products purchased through www.healthylifepress.com.

The Spiritual Fitness Checkup for the 50-Something Woman, by Sharon V. King, PhD – Following the stages of a routine medical exam, the author describes ten spiritual fitness "checkups" midlife women can conduct to assess their spiritual health and tone up their relationship with God. Each checkup consists of the author's personal reflections, a Scripture reference for meditation, and a "Spiritual Pulse Check," with exercises readers can use for personal application. (Printed book: $8.95; PDF eBook: $6.75; both together: $12.95 – direct from publisher; printed books and eBooks available at www.Amazon.com; www.BN.com; www.deepershopping.com, and wherever books are sold.)

The Other Side of Life – Over 60? God Still Has a Plan for You, by Rev. Warren C. Biebel, Jr. – Drawing on biblical examples and his 60-plus years of pastoral experience, Rev. Biebel helps older (and younger) adults understand God's view of aging and the rich life available to everyone who seeks a deeper relationship with God as they age. Rev. Biebel explains how to: Identify God's ongoing plan for your life; Rely on faith to manage the anxieties of aging;  Form positive, supportive relationships; Cultivate patience; Cope with new technologies; Develop spiritual integrity; Understand the effects of dementia; Develop a Christ-centered perspective of aging. (Printed book: $10.95; PDF eBook: $6.95; both together: $15.00 – direct from publisher; printed books and eBooks available at www.Amazon.com; www.BN.com; www.deepershopping.com, and wherever books are sold.)

My Faith, My Poetry, by Gary A. Burlingame – This unique book of Christian poetry is actually two in one. The first collection of poems, A Day in the Life, explores a working parent's daily journey of faith. The reader is carried from morning to bedtime, from "In the Details," to "I Forgot to Pray," back to "Home Base," and finally to "Eternal Love Divine." The second collection of poems, Come Running, is wonder, joy, and faith wrapped up in words that encourage and inspire the mind and the heart. (Printed book: $10.95; PDF eBook: $6.95; both together: $13.95 – direct from publisher; printed books and eBooks available at www.Amazon.com; www.BN.com; www.deepershopping.com, and wherever books are sold.)

On Eagles' Wings, by Sara Eggleston – One woman's life journey from idyllic through chaotic to joy, carried all the way by the One who has promised to never leave us nor forsake us. Remarkable, poignant, moving, and inspiring, this autobiographical account will help many who are facing difficulties that seem too great to overcome or even bear at all. It is proof that Isaiah 40:31 is as true today as when it was penned, "But they that wait upon the LORD shall renew their strength; they shall mount up with wings as eagles; they shall run, and not be weary; and they shall walk, and not faint." (Printed book: $14.95; PDF eBook: $8.95; both together: $22.95 – direct from publisher; printed books and eBooks available at *www.Amazon.com*; *www.BN.com*; *www.deepershopping.com*, and wherever books are sold.)

Richer Descriptions, by Gary A. Burlingame – A unique and handy manual, covering all nine human senses in seven chapters, for Christian speakers and writers. Exercises and a speaker's checklist equip speakers to engage their audiences in a richer experience. Writing examples and a writer's guide help writers bring more life to the characters and scenes of their stories. Bible references encourage a deeper appreciation of being created by God for a sensory existence. (Printed book: $15.95; PDF eBook: $8.95; both together: $22.95 – direct from publisher; printed books and eBooks available at *www.Amazon.com*; *www.BN.com*; *www.deepershopping.com*, and wherever books are sold.)

Treasuring Grace, by Rob Plumley and Tracy Roberts – This novel was inspired by a dream. Liz Swanson's life isn't quite what she'd imagined, but she considers herself lucky. She has a good husband, beautiful children, and fulfillment outside of her home through volunteer work. On some days she doesn't even notice the dull ache in her heart. While she's preparing for their summer kickoff at Lake George, the ache disappears and her sudden happiness is mistaken for anticipation of their weekend. However, as the family heads north, there are clouds on the horizon that have nothing to do with the weather. Only Liz's daughter, who's found some of her mother's hidden journals, has any idea what's wrong. But by the end of the weekend, there will be no escaping the truth or its painful buried secrets.

(Printed: $12.95; PDF eBook: $7.95; both together: $19.95 – direct from publisher; printed books and eBooks available at *www.Amazon.com*; *www.BN.com*; *www.deepershopping.com*, and wherever books are sold.)

From Orphan to Physician – The Winding Path, by Chun-Wai Chan, MD – From the foreword: "In this book, Dr. Chan describes how his family escaped to Hong Kong, how they survived in utter poverty, and how he went from being an orphan to graduating from Harvard Medical School and becoming a cardiologist. The writing is fluent, easy to read and understand. The sequence of events is realistic, emotionally moving, spiritually touching, heartwarming, and thought provoking. The book illustrates . . . how one must have faith in order to walk through life's winding path." (Printed book: $14.95; PDF eBook: $8.95; both together: $22.95 – direct from publisher; printed books and eBooks available at *www.Amazon.com*; *www.BN.com*; *www.deepershopping.com*, and wherever books are sold.)

12 Parables, by Wayne Faust – Timeless Christian stories about doubt, fear, change, grief, and more. Using tight, entertaining prose, professional musician and comedy performer Wayne Faust manages to deal with difficult concepts in a simple, straightforward way. These are stories you can read aloud over and over—to your spouse, your family, or in a group setting. Packed with emotion and just enough mystery to keep you wondering, while

providing lots of points to ponder and discuss when you're through, these stories relate the gospel in the tradition of the greatest speaker of parables the world has ever known, who appears in them often. (Printed book: $14.95; PDF eBook: $8.95; both together: $22.95 – direct from publisher; printed books and eBooks available at *www.Amazon.com*; *www.BN.com*; *www.deepershopping.com*, and wherever books are sold.)

The Answer is Always "Jesus," by Aram Haroutunian, who gave children's sermons for 15 years at a large church in Golden, Colorado—well over 500 in all. This book contains 74 of his most unforgettable presentations—due to the children's responses. Pastors, homeschoolers, parents who often lead family devotions, or other storytellers will find these stories, along with comments about props and how to prepare and present them, an invaluable asset in reconnecting with the simplest, most profound truths of Scripture, and then to envision how best to communicate these so even a child can understand them. (Printed book: $12.95; PDF eBook: $8.95; both together: $19.95 – direct from publisher; printed books and eBooks available at www.Amazon.com; www.BN.com; www.deepershopping.com, and wherever books are sold.)

Handbook of Faith, by Rev. Warren C. Biebel, Jr. – The New York Times World 2011 Almanac claimed that there are 2 billion, 200 thousand Christians in the world, with "Christians" being defined as "followers of Christ." The original 12 followers of Christ changed the world; indeed, they changed the history of the world. So this author, a pastor with over 60 years' experience, poses and answers this logical question: "If there are so many 'Christians' on this planet, why are they so relatively ineffective in serving the One they claim to follow?" Answer: Because, unlike Him, they do not know and trust the Scriptures, implicitly. This little volume will help you do that. (Printed book: $8.95; PDF eBook: $6.95; both together: $13.95 – direct from publisher; printed books and eBooks available at www.Amazon.com; www.BN.com; www.deepershopping.com, and wherever books are sold.)

Pieces of My Heart, by David L. Wood – Eighty-two lessons from normal everyday life. David's hope is that these stories will spark thoughts about God's constant involvement and intervention in our lives and stir a sense of how much He cares about every detail that is important to us. The piece missing represents his son, Daniel, who died in a fire shortly before his first birthday. (Printed book: $16.95; PDF eBook: $8.95; both together: $24.95 – direct from publisher; printed books and eBooks available at www.Amazon.com; www.BN.com; www.deepershopping.com, and wherever books are sold.)

Unless otherwise noted on the site itself, shipping is free for all products purchased through www.healthylifepress.com.

Dream House, by Justa Carpenter – Written by a New England builder of several hundred homes, the idea for this book came to him one day as he was driving that came to him one day as was driving from one job site to another. He pulled over and recorded it so he would remember it, and now you will remember it, too, if you believe, as he does, that "... He who has begun a good work in you will complete it until the day of Jesus Christ." (Printed book: $10.95; PDF eBook: $6.95; both together: $13.95 – direct from publisher; printed books and eBooks available at *www.Amazon.com*; *www.BN.com*; *www.deepershopping.com*, and wherever books are sold.)

A Simply Homemade Clean, by homesteader Lisa Barthuly – "Somewhere along the path, it seems we've lost our gumption, the desire to make things ourselves," says the author. "Gone are the days of 'do it yourself.' Really... why bother? There are a slew of retailers just waiting for us with anything and everything we could need; packaged up all pretty, with no thought or effort required. It is the manifestation of 'progress' ... right?" I don't buy that!" Instead, Lisa describes how to make safe and effective cleansers for home, laundry, and body right in your own home. This saves money and avoids exposure to harmful chemicals often found in commercially produced cleansers. (**Full-color** printed book: $16.99; PDF eBook: $6.95; both together: $22.95 – direct from publisher; printed books and eBooks available at *www.Amazon.com*; *www.BN.com*; *www.deepershopping.com*, and wherever books are sold.)

The Secret of Singing Springs, by Monte Swan – One Colorado family's treasure-hunting adventure along the trail of Jesse James. The Secret of Singing Springs is written to capture for children and their parents the spirit of the hunt—the hunt for treasure as in God's Truth, which is the objective of walking the Way of Wisdom that is described in Proverbs. (Printed book: $12.95, PDF eBook: $9.99; both together: $19.99 – direct from publisher; printed books and eBooks available at *www.Amazon.com*; *www.BN.com*; *www.deepershopping.com*, and wherever books are sold.)

God Loves You Circle, by Michelle Johnson – Daily inspiration for your deeper walk with Christ. This collection of short stories of Christian living will make you laugh, make you cry, but most of all make you contemplate—the meaning and value of walking with the Master moment-by-moment, day-by-day. (**Full-color** printed book: $17.95; PDF eBook: $9.99; both together: $22.99 – direct from publisher; printed books and eBooks available at www.Amazon.com; www.BN.com; www.deepershopping.com, and wherever books are sold.)

Our God-Given Senses, by Gary A. Burlingame – Did you know humans have NINE senses? The Bible draws on these senses to reveal spiritual truth. We are to taste and see that the Lord is a good. We are to carry the fragrance of Christ. Our faith is produced upon hearing. Jesus asked Thomas to touch him. God created us for a sensory experience and that is what you will find in this book. (Printed book: $12.99; PDF eBook: $9.99; both together: $19.99 – direct from publisher; printed books and eBooks available at www.Amazon.com; www.BN.com; www.deepershopping.com, and wherever books are sold.)

Vows, a Romantic novel by F. F. Whitestone – When the police cruiser pulled up to the curb outside, Faith Framingham's heart skipped a beat, for she could see that Chuck, who should have been driving, was not in the vehicle. Chuck's partner, Sandy, stepped out slowly. Sandy's pursed lips and ashen face spoke volumes. Faith waited by the front door, her hands clasped tightly, to counter the fact that her mind was already reeling. "Love never fails." A compelling story. (Printed book: $12.99; PDF eBook: $9.99; both together, $19.99 – direct from publisher; printed books and eBooks available at www.Amazon.com; www.BN.com; www.deepershopping.com, and wherever books are sold.)

Unless otherwise noted on the site itself, shipping is free for all products purchased through www.healthylifepress.com.

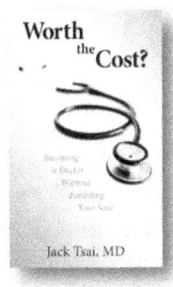

Worth the Cost?, by Jack Tsai, MD – The author was happily on his way to obtaining the American Dream until he decided to take seriously Jesus' command, "Come, follow me." Join him as he explores the cost of medical education and Christian discipleship. Planning to serve God in your future vocation? Take care that your desires do not get side-tracked by the false promises of this world. What you should be doing now so when you are done with your training you will still want to serve God. (Printed book: $12.99, PDF eBook: $9.99; both together: $19.99 – direct from publisher; printed books and eBooks available at www.Amazon.com; www.BN.com; www.deepershopping.com, and wherever books are sold.)

Nature: God's Second Book – An Essential Link to Restoring Your Personal Health and Wellness: Body, Mind, and Spirit, by Elvy P. Rolle – An inspirational book that looks at nature across the seasons of nature and of life. It uses the biblical Emmaus Journey as an analogy for life's journey, and offers ideas for using nature appreciation and exploration to reduce life's stresses. The  author shares her personal story of how she came to grips with this concept after three trips to the emergency room. (**Full-color** printed book: $12.99; PDF eBook $8.99; both together: $16.99 – direct from publisher; printed books and eBooks available at www.Amazon.com; www.BN.com; www.deepershopping.com, and wherever books are sold.)

He Waited, by LaDonna Cooper – Inspires readers to wait upon the Lord for His best for them; stresses the importance of putting God's purpose above one's own; emphasizes that God's love is unconditional; demonstrates the wisdom of waiting, through a combination of positive insights, encouragement, biblical examples and principles. Decorated with original poetry by the author. For singles and others who are waiting. Distributed primarily through www.Amazon.com. (Printed book: $10.99; PDF eBook: $9.99; both together: $15.99 – direct from publisher; printed books and eBooks available at www.Amazon.com; www.BN.com; www.deepershopping.com, and wherever books are sold.)

Seasonal

 **The Big Black Book – What the Christmas Tree Saw,** by Rev. Warren C. Biebel, Jr. – An original Christmas story, from the perspective of the Christmas tree. This little book is especially suitable for parents to read to their children at Christmas time or all year-round. (**Full-color** printed book: $9.95; PDF eBook: $4.95; both together: $12.95 – direct from publisher; printed books and eBooks available at *www.Amazon.com*; *www.BN.com*; *www.deepershopping.com*, and wherever books are sold.)

About Healthy Life Press

Healthy Life Press was founded with a primary goal of helping previously unpublished authors to get their works to market, and to reissue worthy, previously published works that were no longer available. Our mission is to help people toward optimal vitality by providing resources promoting physical, emotional, spiritual, and relational health as viewed from a Christian perspective. We see health as a verb, and achieving optimal health as a process—a crucial process for followers of Christ if we are to love the Lord with all our heart, soul, mind, AND strength, and our neighbors as ourselves—for as long as He leaves us here. We are a collaborative and cooperative small Christian publisher. We share costs/we share proceeds.

For information about publishing with us, e-mail: <u>healthylifepress@aol.com</u>.

www.ingramcontent.com/pod-product-compliance
Lightning Source LLC
Chambersburg PA
CBHW052020070526
44584CB00016B/1836